"Gathering regularly to worship the risen Lord Jesus is essential to the health of the Christian and the health of the church. Without it, we will wither and eventually die spiritually. This book highlights both why we gather and what we do when we gather. Read it with much encouragement and profit."

DANNY AKIN, President,
Southeastern Baptist Theological Seminary

"As a pastor, Tony Merida is giving his life to serving the local church. As a scholar, he uses his considerable gifts to bolster the church and those who serve it, through his teaching and writing ministry. Merida brings the full weight of his experience and gifting together in *Gather*. All who love the church will be encouraged by reading *Gather*, and every local church will be strengthened by applying its message."

JASON ALLEN, President, Midwestern Baptist Theological Seminary; Host, Preaching & Preachers Podcast

"Tony Merida encourages us to move from spectating in directionless comfort to participating with joyful purpose. This book challenges us to reassess our individual motivations for gathering and to realign our hearts with the privilege we have in Christ—to praise and worship our Father God together. The biblical truths outlined in this book will renew our resolve to devote ourselves to our church gatherings (Acts 2:42)."

LUCY LYELL, Chair, London Ministry Wives

"This timely book crackles with energy from cover to cover. The theological vision of church life that it offers is grand and exhilarating, yet it is grounded and practical, down to the value of a good night's sleep on Saturday night! I hope that everyone in the church I pastor will read it, and I am excited to put its lessons into practice in my own life. You could easily read this book in a single sitting—which is great, because it is worth reading over and over."

NICK TUCKER, Vicar, Bishop Hannington Memorial Church, Hove, Suss

Do

D0840022

"With profound clarity, Tony Merida weaves together theological truth and practical wisdom to provide readers with a renewed vision of the beauty and necessity of the local gathering. In a cultural moment when more and more Christians believe they can hold on to Jesus while leaving behind his church, this is the book everyone needs to read!"

ELIZABETH WOODSON, Author, *Embrace Your Life*

"This is a timely and necessary call to all who profess to love Jesus. Tony writes in a way that not only tells me why I need to gather but makes me want to."

ALISTAIR BEGG, Senior Pastor, Parkside Church, Cleveland, Ohio; Bible Teacher, Truth For Life; Author, *Pray Big*

"This book made me look forward to Sunday! Here, you'll find a compelling and highly practical exploration of why we gather each week as God's people."

JONTY ALLCOCK, Pastor, The Globe Church, London; Author, *Impossible Commands*

gather

TONY MERIDA

Gather
Loving Your Church as You Celebrate Christ Together
© 2023 Tony Merida

Published by:
The Good Book Company

thegoodbook.com | thegoodbook.co.uk
thegoodbook.com.au | thegoodbook.co.nz | thegoodbook.co.in

Cover design by Faceout Studio | Art direction and design by André Parker

ISBN: 9781784988272 | Printed in the UK

To Kimberly, my dear companion

"Oh, magnify the LORD with me,
and let us exalt his name together!"
(Psalm 34:3)

CONTENTS

FOREWORD

BY DAVID PLATT

Not long ago, I received a letter from a teenager in our church, who shared the following with me:

Ever since I was little my parents have been separated. My dad is a drug addict and abusive. My first memory with him is a time when I was little and his PO came to my door to do a drug test on him. To make sure he passed the test, he made me urinate in the cup for him. My mom moved around a lot and married into a gang. My life has many different stories that you probably wouldn't believe. My mom died a year and a half ago, and my dad doesn't like me anymore. I lived with my grandma but last year I moved in with my aunt and uncle and that's how I started going to your church. Because of everything going on in my life, I had lost faith in God, and I didn't like going to church. But God's Word being preached here really got through to me and changed my life forever.

This young woman went on to share how she had placed her trust and hope in Jesus as the only one who could save, heal, satisfy, and redeem her, and she was ready to confess her faith in him through baptism.

As I read this letter, I was heartbroken by all the hurt this teenage girl has experienced. At the same time, I was exhilarated by all that happened in her life once she started gathering with our church. Having been let down in so many ways in the world, she had come into our church's gatherings, and through our singing, praying, and preaching, she had discovered the God who will never let her down and a people who assemble to build one another up. By simply being a part of gathered worship, God really "got through" to her, and her life was changed.

Indeed, there is nothing in the world like the gathering of the church. No other meeting or event is like the one that happens week by week when God's people come together in a local church. That is because this gathering, unlike every other gathering in the world, is supernaturally designed by God to edify followers of Jesus and draw people to Jesus while exalting the name of Jesus. In other words, no other gathering is guaranteed by God to lead to our good, to others' good, and to God's glory.

That's why I am so grateful for the book that you hold in your hands, written by a brother and friend whom I love and respect, and I wholeheartedly commend it to you. Whether you are new to faith in Jesus or you've been following Jesus for decades, I am confident that this short book will serve you well. Built upon biblical foundations and filled with practical application, these chapters will help you and others around you experience God's great design for the gathering of his people, particularly in a day when we are tempted in so many ways to diminish or even disregard it altogether.

May the fruit of this book be more and more people coming together before God with all our hurts, pains, struggles, doubts, questions, joys, and sorrows; and may he really "get through" to us in ways that change all our lives and lead to the spread of his glory among all the nations.

David Platt
Pastor-Teacher, McLean Bible Church
August 2022

INTRODUCTION

A RENEWED VISION OF
THE GATHERING

In this book, I want to magnify the priority and privilege of *corporate worship*—that is, believers gathering to worship together in the local church1—and to highlight ways in which, as Christians, we can participate in it for our good, for the good of unbelievers, and for the glory of Christ.2 My hope is that you'll be excited about gathering Sunday by Sunday, and that you'll see how you can contribute to that gathering as well as getting the most from that gathering. To put it another way, this book is not just aiming to motivate you to attend your church's services, but to help you make the most of them when you're there, and to help others make the most of them, too.

---

1 The phrase "corporate worship" may sound like business terminology, but it is taken from the Latin term *corpus* meaning *body*. Thus, it refers to when the body of Christ meets for worship. It may also be called "gathered," "assembled," "public," or "congregational" worship. I will use these terms interchangeably.

2 These ways of participation are selective. I am not attempting to provide a liturgy for churches to follow, but rather attempting to highlight some of the primary features in corporate worship across denominations and throughout time.

This subject is *timeless*, being a central aspect of discipleship. Many of us, I think, have never really stopped to consider the rich significance of corporate worship and the purposes of it, so reflecting on this subject carefully will lead to both joy and growth. But this subject is also *timely*, given the impact of the COVID-19 pandemic. The weekly gathering has been a widely discussed issue, as attendance in gatherings has dropped in many places in the wake of the pandemic. Lots of questions and concerns have been raised about this trend.

To be clear right at the start of this book, attending a church service does not make anyone a Christian. To paraphrase my friend Joby Martin, "Sticking your head in a church building doesn't make you a Christian any more than sticking your head in an oven makes you a biscuit!" Only Jesus saves. He changes us from the inside out. But with that said, the regular gathering of Christians in a local church is one of the primary ways in which we live out our changed lives as faithful disciples of Jesus. A Christian is marked not only by a love for Christ but also by a love for his people (1 John 3:14). The New Testament knows nothing of "lone-ranger Christianity." Our faith is personal, but it is not individualistic. God wants us to live our faith out in community in church, and regularly gathering for worship and instruction is at the heart of this idea.

THERE'S NOTHING GREATER THAT WE COULD DO TOGETHER

For several years, our church (Imago Dei Church in Raleigh, North Carolina) helped support a church plant in Frankfurt, Germany, which was led by a pastor named Stephan Pues. On one visit to our church, Stephan was able to join us for corporate worship (we met in a storefront at that time), but because his flight left on Monday morning, I was unable to show him round our city. I said sadly to Stephan, "Man, I'm sorry. I wish we had some more time together. I would love to show you some of my favorite restaurants and some of my favorite sites." Stephan, who is not the dramatic type, responded:

> *There's nothing greater that we could have done together. There's nothing greater that you could have shown me. I just got to worship with the saints at Imago Dei Church. We got to enjoy the end for which we are created together.*

He was right, and he'd remembered what I'd forgotten: *there is nothing greater than gathering to worship with the church family*. Nothing.

The problem is, many of us don't actually live like that. For some, gathering is fine if you have nothing else to do on a Sunday. For others, travel, sports, and other activities are given priority over it. In recent years, many have preferred watching the livestream in their pajamas rather than going through the hassle of showing up physically. Others reason that since you can worship

God in the beauty of nature, then going to the lake or the mountains is of equal value to gathering with the saints.

Maybe some of that resonates with you. Maybe for you, even if you don't see it as an optional extra, church on a Sunday is a duty to fulfill, not a delight to anticipate. What will make all of us like Stephan? Only a renewed vision of corporate worship. So let me take you straight to a remarkable passage in Hebrews 12, where the writer says:

> *But you have come to Mount Zion and to the city of the living God, the heavenly Jerusalem, and to innumerable angels in festal gathering, and to the assembly of the firstborn who are enrolled in heaven, and to God, the judge of all, and to the spirits of the righteous made perfect, and to Jesus, the mediator of a new covenant, and to the sprinkled blood that speaks a better word than the blood of Abel .... Therefore let us be grateful for receiving a kingdom that cannot be shaken, and thus let us offer to God acceptable worship, with reverence and awe, for our God is a consuming fire.*
>
> *(Hebrews 12:22-24, 28-29)*

Don't miss what he's saying: when we gather for corporate worship, not only do we join with millions of brothers and sisters around the world, but we also join a heavenly worship service that is already happening, and that one day we ourselves will stand in! As Edmund Clowney says, "In corporate worship we rise by faith to enter the heavenly assembly of the saints and angels"[3] to worship with gratitude the God who is gracious to sinners and with great gravity before the God who is a consuming fire. In other words, there is more going on than meets the eye in our gatherings.

All of us gather in community. It's part of being human and always has been. We gather for a whole host of reasons: football games, political protests, pop concerts, and more. People will show up early, stay late, express themselves passionately, spend loads of money, and drive great distances to attend these events. But they all pale in comparison with the glorious gathering of God's people. These events are enjoyable, but they cannot be anything other than temporary and fleeting, and they cannot ultimately fulfill us. None of them carry the significance of the people of God assembled for worship.

LET US EXALT HIS NAME TOGETHER

In light of this, it should be no surprise that the New Testament continually emphasizes the importance and goodness of God's people gathering. The earliest snapshot of the church conveys this moving image of the church gathered. Following Peter's preaching of the gospel on the day of Pentecost, about 3,000 people were converted and baptized: "And they devoted themselves to

---

3 Edmund P. Clowney, "Corporate Worship: A Means of Grace," *Give Praise to God*, edited by Philip Graham Ryken, Derek W.H. Thomas, and J. Ligon Duncan III (P&R, 2003), p 96.

the apostles' teaching and the fellowship, to the breaking of bread and the prayers" (Acts 2:42). Throughout Acts, believers gathered together for worship and instruction. In his epistles, Paul refers to the gathering on numerous occasions because it is intrinsic to the Christian life: "When [not if] you come together as a church..." he writes to the Corinthians (1 Corinthians 11:18). The writer of Hebrews warns Christians of the danger of "neglecting to meet together" (Hebrews 10:25).

In this, the New Testament is simply carrying on what we see among the people of God in the Old Testament. The phrase "meet[ing] together" in Hebrews 10:25 is the word *episynagōgē*. You can hear the old word "synagogue" in it (where a Jewish assembly met for worship and teaching). And the word for "church" is taken from the Old Testament term for "assembly" (*ekklēsia* in Greek). A church is an *assembling*. It is, of course, more than that, but it's never less. Throughout redemptive history God's people have assembled. There are numerous Old Testament examples of the saints gathered (see Deuteronomy 9:10; Judges 20:2; 1 Kings 8:14; 1 Chronicles 28:8; Nehemiah 8:1-2). The Psalms highlight this privilege and priority:

Oh, magnify the LORD with me,
and let us exalt his name together! (Psalm 34:3)

Oh come, let us worship and bow down;
let us kneel before the LORD, our Maker!
For he is our God,

> *and we are the people of his pasture,*
> *and the sheep of his hand. (Psalm 95:6-7)*

The Psalms of Ascent portray God's people singing on their way to Jerusalem to worship God together during festival seasons (Psalms 120 – 134).

This is what God's people have always done: they exalt their Redeemer *together*. I know church gatherings may not look as impressive as pop concerts or sports events or political rallies. Believers gathered in a small building, in a storefront, in a house, or even in a beautiful church building can look less than spectacular. But this is why we must assess things in a biblical way rather than a worldly way. Though the psalmist had the Old Testament temple rather than the new-covenant church in mind, his words have application for the church's gathering:

> *For a day in your courts is better*
> *than a thousand elsewhere.*
> *I would rather be a doorkeeper in the house of my God*
> *than dwell in the tents of wickedness. (Psalm 84:10)*

There is nothing greater. And I have to ask myself: do I believe this? How can my heart catch up with my theology? I know I need to rehearse something like this on some Sunday mornings: "Better is one day in your courts, oh Lord, than sitting on the front row on the third base side at Nationals Park watching the Nationals play a baseball game." You can insert your own favorite place or activity.

JESUS IS IN OUR MIDST

There are two more truths that we need to work into our hearts if we are to believe that there is nothing greater than gathering as church. The first is that when we assemble as his people, Jesus is present with us by his Spirit in a particularly powerful way. Of course you can worship God anywhere, but there is something special about the corporate assembly. It is "the household of God," built on "Christ Jesus himself [as] the cornerstone, in whom the whole structure, being joined together, grows into a holy temple in the Lord ... into a dwelling place for God by the Spirit" (Ephesians 2:19-22).

One writer puts it this way:

As the church is being renewed today, Jesus' grace and glory are especially being experienced in worship. Like Israel of old, as we gather in His name and direct our sustained praises to Him (not just about Him), His Spirit descends and His presence is manifest in our midst. Jesus is here.[4]

You simply cannot experience this anywhere else. Richard Foster puts it succinctly: "When we are truly gathered into worship, things occur that could never occur alone."[5]

---

4 Don Williams, "Psalms 73-150" in *The Preacher's Commentary* (Thomas Nelson, Kindle Edition, 1989), Kindle locations 2290-2292.

5 Richard Foster, *Celebration of Discipline* (Harper Collins, 1998), p 164.

Then second, the local assembly is a preview of the glory to come. In fact, the temple served as a "copy" of heaven itself (Hebrews 8:1-5), where all the redeemed will be gathered and finally at home (Revelation 21 – 22). It contained echoes of the Garden of Eden and pointed ahead to paradise being restored. All of history is moving to the climactic moment of all believers being gathered around the throne, worshiping together with worshipers from every tribe, people, language, and nation (5:9). No other gathering under heaven compares to this reality. When we gather together, we are being given—and we are experiencing—a glimpse of that future gathering in the new heavens and the new earth.

All of this is a result of the gracious initiative of God, who has drawn us to Christ by the power of the Spirit and has transformed us. A result of true conversion is a *change in affections*. Old loves have been replaced by a superior, all-satisfying love for Jesus. And the desire to express adoration to him, alongside other brothers and sisters purchased by his blood, is the result of the regenerating and renewing work of the Holy Spirit. So, as you begin to read this book, do be praying. Ask God to work in you by his Spirit so that in joyful worship of his Son, you are able to say of your church gathering, unspectacular though it may look in the eyes of the world, "There is nothing greater". That is the path to seeing it as a privilege and making it a priority, not as duty but as delight.

1. THE GIFT
OF GATHERING

Let us draw near with a true heart in full assurance
of faith, with our hearts sprinkled clean from an evil
conscience and our bodies washed with pure water.
Hebrews 10:24

I t is remarkable that we are able to worship God together at all. In Hebrews 10:19-25, the writer concisely describes how God makes worshipers in the first place: through *the gracious work of Christ*. To even be able to worship God is a divine privilege of grace. Apart from Jesus, though we may attend a gathering, we are on the outside of what is really going on:

*Therefore, brothers, since we have confidence to enter the holy places **by the blood of Jesus**, by the new and living way that he opened for us through the curtain, that is, through his flesh, and since we have a great priest over the house of God, let us draw near with a true heart **in full assurance of faith**, with our hearts sprinkled clean from an evil conscience and our bodies washed with pure water. Let us hold fast the confession of our hope without* *wavering, for he who promised is faithful. And let us consider how to stir up one another to love and good works, not neglecting to meet together, as is the habit of some, but encouraging one another, and all the more as you see the Day drawing near. (Hebrews 10:19-25)*

This is a crucial text for us as we think about gathering, and it makes three main exhortations, the first two of which we will look at in this chapter, and the third of which we'll enjoy in chapter 2:

- Let us draw near to God.

- Let us hold fast to our confession.

- Let us consider how to stir up one another.

But these exhortations do not come out of nowhere. They are *responses to the work of Christ on behalf of sinners* (v 19-21). Jesus' work, and Jesus' work alone, enables and motivates our worship and obedience. Jesus has given us access to God. It is because of what Jesus has done for us that we can respond in *faith* (v 22), *hope* (v 23), and *love* (v 24). It is because of what Jesus has done for us that we can gather with confidence to worship the God who is present with us.

WORSHIP AS A RESPONSE TO CHRIST'S WORK

Why is it that you and I can so confidently enter the presence of the perfect, awesome God, who is a "consuming fire"? It is certainly not because of our own performance! Believers have confidence to enter the presence of God not based on our works but based on Christ's work on our behalf. As the hymn writer put it:

Before the throne of God above
I have a strong and perfect plea;
A great High Priest, whose name is Love,
Who ever lives and pleads for me.

My name is graven on his hands,
My name is written on his heart.
I know that while in heaven he stands
No tongue can bid me thence depart,
No tongue can bid me thence depart.

When Satan tempts me to despair
And tells me of the guilt within,
Upward I look and see him there
Who made an end to all my sin.[6]

When we consider afresh what Christ has done for us— when we feel his love deeply in our hearts and when we revel in our new standing before God—then the instinct is to worship God. A failure to prioritize or enjoy the gathering of God's people is often tied to the failure to apply such rich gospel truths to our hearts. Which means that the time when you and I most need to attend the corporate gathering is when we do not feel like it! It is in those times that we most need other Christians to sing and speak and show the gospel to us. In his classic

---

6 Charitie Lees Bancroft, "Before the Throne of God Above," https://hymnary.org/text/before_the_throne_of_god_above_i_have_a_ (accessed Dec. 16, 2022).

book *Life Together*, Dietrich Bonhoeffer, a persecuted Christian in Nazi Germany, had this to say:

> *The Christian needs another Christian who speaks God's Word to him. He needs him again and again when he becomes uncertain and discouraged ... The Christ in his own heart is weaker than the Christ in the word of his brother; his own heart is uncertain, his brother's is sure. And that also clarifies the goal of all Christian community: they meet one another as bringers of the message of salvation ... Their fellowship is founded solely upon Jesus Christ.*[7]

You have the privilege not only of drawing near to God in worship through the finished work of Jesus but also of reminding your brothers and sisters of the gospel through your words of encouragement, your singing, and your prayers.

Consider afresh the privilege: *we can draw near to God*. No worshiper in the old covenant would have been bold enough to attempt entry into the Most Holy Place, the dwelling place of God in the heart of the temple. Only the high priest could do that, and only once a year. To use a slightly flippant illustration, in the movie *Fast and Furious 9*, the characters Tej and Roman go to space in a little souped-up, rocket-propelled Pontiac Fiero (by the ninth film, the writers had left realism far behind!). It

---

7 Dietrich Bonhoeffer, *Life Together* (Harper One, 1954), p 23.

is a humorous scene. They are like, "No way man. How'd we get here? What are we doing here?" As Christians we should ask an even more astounding question: "How did we get access to the Most Holy Place? How is it that we can gather and have God be present among us and look forward to the day when we will be in the very presence of God?" Answer: Jesus. You have a better chance of going into space in a Pontiac Fiero than of getting into the Most Holy Place apart from Jesus!

Jesus gave us this access because he made a way "through the curtain" (Hebrews 10:20). This curtain is an allusion to the separation of the outer and inner rooms of the tabernacle/temple, pointing to a greater heavenly reality: a barrier one must pass to enter God's presence. It has been opened through Christ's atoning work on the cross, when the temple's curtain was torn from top to bottom, giving access. Our confidence to enter God's presence is not in our résumé, our status, or our religious efforts. It is due to Jesus' finished work. And therefore, we want to gather; the liberated people of God want to exult in the grace of God together.

LET US DRAW NEAR TO GOD

So corporate worship should aim to exalt God, and this brings joy to God's people. We go wrong when we aim for the second without majoring on the first; that is, we do not gather for entertainment but for exaltation. On one occasion, someone told the pastor Francis Chan that they did not like the worship service very much, to which he quipped, "That's ok—we weren't worshiping you." Cheeky, but true. It is always as we see Christ, and appreciate his love for us, that we will both be moved to worship him and given confidence that we can worship him. So our worship is to be done with "full assurance of faith" (Hebrews 10:22b). To get the most out of worship, remind yourself of what Christ has done for you and draw near with full assurance. Because of the work of Christ, you do not have to be tentative in worshiping God. In Christ, we are welcomed—so let us worship him in Spirit-empowered freedom and joy. Equally, the work of Christ means we worship *wholeheartedly*. The writer says that we should draw near to God "with a true heart" (v 22). A true or "sincere" heart is a heart that is in the right place. There is an important connection between truth and the heart. God does not want an empty-headed emotionalism (because truth matters). But God also does not want an empty-hearted intellectualism (because the heart matters). So we are to draw near *sincerely* and *passionately*. Our gatherings should be full of truth and of joy.

EVERYONE WORSHIPS

The privilege of worshiping God because of what Christ has done on our behalf actually answers the great question that every human is (subconsciously, often) asking: *who will I worship?* Everyone worships something or someone. The American writer David Foster Wallace, himself by no means a Christian, once said in a commencement speech at Kenyon College:

Everybody worships. The only choice we get is what to worship. And the compelling reason for maybe choosing some sort of god … to worship … is that pretty much anything else you worship will eat you alive. If you worship money and things, if they are where you tap real meaning in life, then you will never have enough, never feel you have enough. It's the truth. Worship your own body and beauty and sexual allure, and you will always feel ugly. And when time and age start showing, you will die a million deaths before [your loved ones] finally plant you … Worship power, and you will end up feeling weak and afraid, and you will need ever more power over others to numb you to your own fear. Worship your intellect, being seen as smart, you will end up feeling stupid, a fraud, always on the verge of being found out. Look, the insidious thing about these forms of worship is not that they are evil or sinful; it is that they're unconscious. They are default settings.[8]

Our default setting is that we are wired for worship. Not only that, but we are wired for community (which is why there is something so compelling about being in the crowd at a sports game or being part of a political rally—there is an object of worship, and we are worshiping in community[9]).

---

8 David Foster Wallace, "This Is Water," quoted in Micah Fries, *Exalting Jesus in Zephaniah, Haggai, Zechariah, Malachi* (Nashville: B&H, 2015), p 50.

9 This is not at all to say that enjoying attending a sports game or political meeting is by definition wrong or idolatrous. But look around you at these events—plenty of people are making a "god" out of a leader they look to to make everything right, or

The truth is that our hearts will never be satisfied until we come to know and worship the God who made us. Worshiping him is an all-satisfying privilege. As the 5th-century church father Augustine prayed, "You stir man to take pleasure in praising you, because you have made us for yourself, and our heart is restless until it rests in you."[10] And so, when we praise God in community—in the gathering—we are doing what we are made for: worshiping in community. We are saved into a community, and the gathering makes our identity with the family of God visible and delightful. God did not save us so that we could go to heaven as individuals, apart from each other, but as individuals who are part of a holy community. Christianity is personal, but it is not individualistic.

LET US HOLD FAST TO OUR CONFESSION OF HOPE

Sandwiched between the exhortations to draw near to God and to consider how we may stir up one another is this exhortation: "Let us hold fast to the confession of our hope without wavering, for he who promised is faithful" (Hebrews 10:23). In other words, in light of what Jesus has done, *persevere in hope*.

The New Testament's understanding of *hope* is not wishful thinking, but rather, settled confidence centered

---

a sports team they look to for identity and victory.

10 Augustine, *Confessions*. Translated with an Introduction and Notes by Henry Chadwick (Oxford University Press, 1991), p 3.

on the coming of Jesus. Christians are to persevere in hope with their eyes on Jesus (12:1-2). The "confession" in view is our public confession of the gospel, by which we are brought into that confident hope that Jesus will return to make all things new and that we will live with him. And when we suffer or are persecuted (as the recipients of Hebrews were being), we need to be reminded of our hope, grounded in the truth that God keeps his promises. One of the primary places where we are reminded of those promises of God, and where we are therefore refilled with gospel hope, is *in the assembly of God's people*, as the gospel is sung, declared, and seen in baptism and in the Lord's Supper.

Why attend the corporate gathering? *Because life is hard, and we need hope.* It is this hope that will inspire a life of faithfulness. We need the gathering so that we can press on in the face of difficulties. We do not attend because we are better than others or have life sorted out, but as people in need of Jesus' grace to forgive us as sinners and to strengthen us as sufferers. By attending the gathering, we are in a sense saying, "I need help. I need support. I need accountability. I need hope."

We should never imagine that the believers who attend our gatherings are devoid of trials. Each week, I know I am surrounded by people who are dealing with things like miscarriages, failed adoptions, loss of jobs, terrible jobs, family conflicts, addictions, upcoming surgeries, anxiety, doubt, and more. And I bring my own trials and disappointments and regrets in through the door, too. We need one another to persevere in hope. We need to hear our brothers and sisters sing; we need the prayers of God's people; we need to hear the gospel heralded; we need to taste and see that the Lord is good in the Lord's Supper; and we need to give and receive encouragement to and from other redeemed sinners and sufferers.

As Bonhoeffer reflected on the privilege of gathering with God's people, he wrote:

> *It is by the grace of God that a congregation is permitted to gather visibly in this world to share God's Word and sacrament. Not all Christians receive this blessing. The imprisoned, the sick, the scattered lonely, the proclaimers of the Gospel in heathen lands stand alone. They know that visible fellowship is a blessing ... The physical presence of other Christians is a source of incomparable joy and strength to the believer ... The prisoner, the sick person, the Christian in exile sees in the companionship of a fellow Christian a physical sign of the gracious presence of the triune God ... It is grace, nothing but grace, that we are allowed to live in community with Christian brethren.*[11]

It is because of the kindness of God in Christ, and only because of that kindness, that you enjoy the privilege of worshiping God corporately as you gather as the redeemed people of God, en route to your heavenly home. It is

---

11 Bonhoeffer, *Life Together*, p 18-19.

literally what you were made for—to enjoy worshiping God in the community of his people, in his presence.

ACTION STEPS

Of course there are times when you must miss a gathering due to sickness, work, being deployed for some kind of service, being on mission, or being vulnerable to disease. But ordinarily, we make every effort not just to be present at weekly worship but to make it special. How may we do this?

- *Get adequate sleep on Saturday night.* I know the appeal of movies, socializing, and sports on Saturdays, and I am not saying we should always avoid these pleasures. They can be sources of rest and enjoyment. However, if you were going to have a big meeting for work the next day, would you not do all you could to get sufficient rest the night before? If we truly believe that the Sunday gathering is the high point of the week, then we should prepare accordingly.

- *Read the sermon passage ahead of time.* Perhaps you can do this on Saturday night with your family; or on Sunday morning before heading out to church; or upon arrival at church. Reading ahead of the sermon will put you in a good frame of mind when it is time for the message.

- *Pray for your leaders.* Pray for their spiritual well-being. Pray for their families. Pray for the conflicts they are dealing with. Pray for their faithfulness to God. Pray for their hearts to be enlarged for God's people. Pray for the Spirit to move mightily through them so that lives are changed.

- *Pray for fellow members and those visiting.* Pray that the gathering would be a means of instruction and encouragement to members. Pray that unbelievers would be drawn to Christ and become his followers. Pray for the kids in the church: that they would be captivated by Jesus at a young age and would follow him all their days in love and adoration.

- *Consider having some special traditions on Sundays.* Perhaps that is a meal with your family. Perhaps that involves inviting people over for a meal. Perhaps it is a family walk later in the day. Or perhaps it involves slowly reading through a good Christian book in the evening. Allow this day of worship to be a means of nourishing yourself for the week ahead.

2. GATHERING TO STIR UP ONE ANOTHER

And let us consider how to stir up one another to love and good works, not neglecting to meet together, as is the habit of some, but encouraging one another, and all the more as you see the Day drawing near.
Hebrews 10:24-25

COVID-19 has forced us all to think and talk about the gathering theologically and practically. It has caused conflict and forced some awkward conversations. You may have been surprised by how much you missed gathering in person, or by how little you did. In challenging seasons and confusing times, it is easy to say, "Boy, I wish we could go back to the early church. Things were simpler in the 1st century."

But not so fast.

While we may not read of the impact of a global pandemic back then, we do read of the problem of *absenteeism* in the corporate assembly. This is not a new issue.

MEETING TOGETHER

Hebrews is one long exhortation to endure in faith to the end and not to drift away. In alignment with this exhortation, the writer makes a strong appeal to prioritize the regular assembly of the church—because it is one of the graces that God gives us to enable long-term faithfulness. Attendance matters because perseverance in the faith matters.

Apparently, forsaking the assembly had become a "habit" for some of these early believers. Why? What had prompted their absence? Scholars have offered several possible reasons, but the most likely was persecution. So then, the writer is saying, *Gather together regularly **even if it brings persecution***. The gathering of the saints is *that* important.

This puts the contemporary inconveniences of Western Christians into perspective. Most professing believers in the West today who do not prioritize gathering weekly are not forsaking the assembly because they fear persecution. Rather, we stop because of a preoccupation with other things or unmet preferences over trivial things.[12] There is no shortage of excuses when it comes

---

12 Scholar William Lane notes that this was the problem in 2nd-century Rome: "It is natural to think that the neglect of the meetings was motivated by fear of recognition by outsiders in a time of persecution, or by disappointment of the delay of the Parousia, or by some other acute concern. It is sobering to discover that in the early second century in Rome it was simply preoccupation with business affairs that accounted for the neglect of the meetings of a house church." William L. Lane, *Hebrews 9-13 Word Biblical Commentary* (Word Books, 1991), p 290.

to why Christians miss their church's gathering, but for 99% of us in the West, none of them is "persecution."

As many have pointed out through the years, our habits form our life rhythms and shape our loves. Binge watching Netflix habitually will shape you; going to the gym daily will (literally) shape you; and not attending the gathering of God's people will shape you. And the flipside is also true. When you habitually gather with believers to sing, pray, recite your beliefs, hear God's word, take the bread and the wine, observe baptisms, and encourage one another, it will have a shaping impact on your life, and so it is essential for your spiritual endurance.

WHY NOT JUST WATCH AT HOME?

Several years ago, I remember asking my congregation, "Why attend corporate worship when you could just snuggle up with a box of chocolates and a coffee and read a Charles Spurgeon sermon? After all, his sermons are better than mine, right?" I had no idea how relevant that question would be in 2020–2021—simply with "watch sermons" replacing "read a sermon." It is a live question for a YouTube streaming generation. So, why not simply tune in from home? The writer of Hebrews gives one answer, but before we see what he says, it is first worth pointing out something about the importance of *physical embodiment*. There is something special about being gathered physically. While technology can be used in a supplemental way to enhance our faith, it will never be a substitute for real physical presence.

Think about the incarnation: "The Word became flesh and dwelt among us" (John 1:14). Jesus did not "zoom" us from heaven. He came among us. He could be seen, touched, and heard (1 John 1:1-2). The incarnation is about embodiment.

Further, believers are anticipating a *bodily* resurrection when Jesus returns bodily and visibly, and we will dwell together in a new creation with glorified bodies. We are made for real embodiment.

John tells us that there are limits to pen and ink (or for us, texting, email, and video messaging): "Though I have much to write to you, I would rather not use paper and ink. Instead I hope to come to you and talk face to face, *so that our joy may be complete*" (2 John v 12, my emphasis; see also 3 John v 13-14). Notice how he states his desire for face-to-face interaction. Why? To complete their joy. Something is clearly lacking without physical interaction, and one of those things is the presence of deep and abiding joy. A lack of embodied gathering must result in a lack of real fellowship with other Christians, which will lead to a loss of joy. We are in need of embodied relationships.

LET US STIR UP ONE ANOTHER

It's significant that the action linked to not forsaking the gathering in Hebrews 10:24-25 is not preaching or singing or praying, but rather *stirring up one another to love and good deeds* (v 24—which is a subset of "encouraging one another" in verse 25). While preaching and singing should do these things, the focus is not on a worship leader or preacher but on the congregation actively stirring one another up.

We need this—we need to "encourage each other daily, while it is still called today, so that none of you is hardened by sin's deception" (Hebrews 3:12-13, CSB). And one of the primary places for this mutual encouragement is in our church gatherings. As Ray Ortlund has said on his *You're Not Crazy* podcast, "no one is over-encouraged," so it is not hard to find someone who needs to be encouraged in your fellowship! Perhaps one of the reasons why the popular show *Ted Lasso* has gained quite a following is that it features a coach who is a constant encourager, and the practice of steady encouragement is uncommon in today's hostile and divided age. But it should be the normal practice for Christians.

Your presence in corporate worship matters, then, because you have a part to play in encouraging your brothers and sisters and provoking them to love and good deeds. These are not our natural inclinations; we need to be stirred up to genuinely care for others and to perform selfless acts for others. One important purpose of fellowship, then, is to keep each other from turning inward on ourselves, becoming self-centered and self-absorbed, which not only harms the unity and purpose of the church but also brings a profound sense of joylessness to such a person. These person-to-person interactions simply cannot be replicated by watching a worship service virtually. Life-on-life care for one another matters more than many of us realize. We need a strong dose of Hebrews 10:24-25.

Of course, this does not mean that showing up at the gathering checks the "encouragement" box. It is easy to subconsciously adopt this kind of attitude: "I arrive just after the service begins. I leave when it's over. I don't really interact with anyone, nor do I care to do so. Give me a decent sermon that doesn't bore me, and I'm all good." The writer of Hebrews simply will not allow this attitude—because mutual building up cannot happen in this way.

In today's consumeristic world, our natural question is "What can I get out of worship?" The Bible commands us to replace it with a different one: "What encouragement can I give to others?"

Do not miss the implicit warning in this text when it is viewed in light of the whole book of Hebrews, where apostasy is mentioned. William Lane states, "The writer regarded the desertion of the communal meetings as utterly serious. It threatened the corporate life of the congregation and almost certainly was *a prelude to apostasy* on the part of those who were separating themselves from the assembly."[13] A failure to take the gathering seriously was "symptomatic of a catastrophic

---

13 Lane, p 290, my emphasis.

failure to appreciate the significance of Christ's priestly ministry and the access to God it provided."[14] Your attendance or lack of attendance is saying something about your heart, about your response to Christ's atoning work, and about your belief in the coming "Day of the Lord" (v 25). It matters for you, as well as for others, that you do not forsake the assembly.

THREE TRUTHS ON ENCOURAGING

Hopefully by now you're persuaded of the need to be physically present in your church services in order to encourage others to keep going, to love, and to do good works. Here are three ways you can be lovingly inciting others to persevere in the faith.

First, it is the result of careful thought. We need to "consider" (v 24)—to give attention to the matter. Pay attention to the hurts and burdens and temptations of others. Pastor Richard Phillips says, "This is not an invitation for us to be judgmental busybodies, making the lives of others a burden. But it does mandate that we take a lively interest in the affairs of other believers."[15] Faithful church members take a lively interest in one another so that they can be effective in seeking to make their burdens lighter.

Giving encouragement is like giving gifts. Good gift-givers pay attention to the interests of others, and they

---

14 Lane, p 290.

15 Richard D. Phillips, *Hebrews* (P&R, 2006), p 364.

give thoughtful gifts as a result. Faithful encouragers consider carefully how they may edify others, knowing that each person is different. Encouragement is not one-size-fits-all. You may encourage others by letting them know you are praying for them (if, in fact, you are!); by sharing a passage of Scripture with them that may be timely for them; by giving them a gift and a good word to go along with it; or by simply thinking about a clear and thoughtful statement that will build them up.

People change, and circumstances change, so this means the ministry of encouragement never ends, and it can take many different shapes and forms, with Christ always being central in this ministry. When preparing to gather with the saints, think about who you could encourage, and how you may encourage them. Pray for God to show you someone whom you can encourage once you arrive.

Second, it is the responsibility of all of God's people. Notice the writer says, "Let *us*..." (v 24, my emphasis). The ministry of stirring up one another is not for "elite super Christians" or just for extroverts. It is for Christians. This means we are to assume some responsibility for the joy and growth of those in our fellowship.

I became a follower of Christ in college, and I remember it was very common to hear and use the phrase, "Christianity is about a personal relationship with Jesus." And at one level this is true. Christianity is personal; as Paul says, "Christ loved me and gave himself for me" (Galatians 2:20). But it is also about having new relationships with those who, in Christ, are our brothers and sisters. We have a lot of "me and Jesus" Christianity, and there is a great need for more "we and Jesus" community. If you are a Christian, the encouragement of others in your church is your responsibility.

Third, it is to be practiced in view of the final Day. The writer, underlining the importance of this ministry of encouragement, speaks of a "Day" that is approaching: the ultimate day of judgment and salvation. This reality should give us added reason to spur our brothers and sisters on to persevere.

The Protestant Reformer Martin Luther reportedly once quipped, "There are two days on my calendar; this day and that Day." If you live thinking only about the next pay raise, or sporting event, or home improvement project, or vacation, you will not feel this urgency. Live with the kind of heavenly awareness that Luther did and not only will you be at the weekly gathering of your church, but you will be there with a purpose: you will seek to stir up your fellow saints as you walk together on your journey to the new creation. You need no official position, specified level of Bible knowledge, or particular personality to do this; and remember, no one can ever be encouraged too much.

ACTION STEPS

- *Recognize that there will be times in which you do not feel like attending corporate worship, but do not let that feeling keep you away.* Allow that to actually drive you to the fellowship. One of our church members, Tom, told me recently, "Sometimes I come to church in a bad mood. But when we recite the creed out loud, it lifts me up and renews my heart and mind." Do not let your mood keep you from the assembly. Come as you are.

- *Remember that there will be people present who did not feel like turning up.* Do not expect everyone to be happy on Sunday. Life is hard. Be sensitive to the heavy-hearted, seek prayerfully to spot them, and aim to gladden them with a good word (Proverbs 12:25).

- *Do not minimize the importance of gospel-centered conversations.* Ordinarily on Sunday afternoon my wife will ask me, "Did you have any good conversations with people?" Rarely does she ask me much about the sermon or the music— she knows that a lot of ministry takes place in conversational times. In your conversations, aim not only to talk about work and the weather and the kids, but to be open and to ask questions that engage with someone spiritually, and to give gospel-centered encouragement.

Remember that a wise, well-chosen word can have a tremendous impact.

- *Try to arrive early and stay late.* Be on the lookout for someone that you can encourage in the gospel; or perhaps seek them out so that they may encourage you, as you relate to them your trials and concerns.

3. GATHERING TO HEAR GOD'S WORD

Until I come, devote yourself to the public reading of Scripture, to exhortation, to teaching.
1 Timothy 4:13

The popular American agnostic professor Bart Ehrman tells of an annual scene in one of his classes at the University of North Carolina, Chapel Hill. Ehrman asks his large class three questions. First question: "How many of you believe that the Bible is the inspired word of God?" Usually, a high percentage of students raise their hands. Second question: "How many of you have read [insert a popular author's latest book]?" Virtually everyone raises his or her hand. And then the final question: "How many of you have read the entire Bible?" And almost no one raises a hand.

Professor Ehrman points out the obvious problem, saying, "I understand why you would want to read [such and such popular author], but *if you really believe God wrote a book, wouldn't you want to read it?*"

If we believe God wrote a book, should this not change everything? Paul Tripp drills down deep into what it should look like to believe this:

> *Well, if you really believe that the Bible is the word of God, preserved by God for you, wouldn't it be the most valuable, esteemed, treasured, and well-used possession in your life? Would you not love the moments when you could sit with it, read it carefully, study its content, and meditate on its implications? Wouldn't you commit yourself to be an avid reader and lifelong student of the word of God? Wouldn't you work to be sure that you have understood and interpreted it correctly? Wouldn't you treasure the teachers and preachers whom God has raised up to walk you through his word? Wouldn't you want to make sure that everything you desire, think, say, and do was done in joyful submission and careful obedience to the word of God?*[16]

There is nothing like the word of God. We have a God who speaks to us, and so an essential—not to say exciting—aspect of our gatherings is to hear his word faithfully preached. It is a gift of grace that we are able to come together to hear God speak to us in his word.

HEARING GOD'S WORD PREACHED

The goal of all preaching in corporate worship is the same as every other aspect of the gathering: to exalt

---

16 Paul Tripp, *Do You Believe?* (Crossway, 2021), p 41.

Christ. Hearing God's word preached to us does not happen *after* worship. It *is* worship. The whole of Scripture speaks to us of the Lord Jesus (Luke 24:27, 44-45), and so good preaching exposes the meaning of a biblical text and points people from that text to Christ, so that they may know him, worship him, and obey him. So, when you listen to a sermon, remember that God has not given you this gift in order to leave you excited by the oratory or with a better explanation of the text, but to leave you in awe of who Jesus is and how he loves his people. If you have a preacher who does this, give God thanks!

In some contexts today, preaching is downplayed. Much more time is devoted to singing than to preaching in some churches. In other contexts, a lot of time is given to preaching but the sermons lack biblical depth and gospel focus. That is a challenge to church leaders, but as church members, we need to challenge ourselves too: do we give the same degree of attention to hearing the word as we do to the other elements of worship? It's easy to sing our hearts out, to enjoy the fellowship of our church family, to be grateful that our kids are engaged by the kids' ministry... but to allow ourselves to zone out during the sermon or to forget what we were shown of Jesus and his call on our lives straight after the preaching has finished. Imagine talking to your friend or your spouse and then putting your fingers in your ears when it is their turn to talk, or listening in such a half-hearted way that five minutes later you have forgotten what they shared with you. That would not go well! Likewise, be sure not only to praise God for faithful, Christ-exalting preaching but to pray that the Spirit will help you listen to it, respond to it, and remember and be changed by it.

HEARING GOD'S WORD PREACHED: THE PATTERN IN PUBLIC WORSHIP

Right from the start, Christians have prioritized the exposition of Scripture in their assemblies. After talking about public prayer in corporate worship (1 Timothy 2:1-8), Paul has this to say about the public reading and exposition of Scripture in corporate worship: "Until I come, devote yourself to the public reading of Scripture, to exhortation, to teaching" (4:13). R. Kent Hughes comments, "This simple sentence is a landmark text in defining the major work of the pastor and the worship of the church."[17] This verse highlights biblical authority, and it displays a biblical pattern of exposition in corporate worship.

The word translated with the English phrase "public reading of Scripture" (*anagnōsis*) means to read aloud in public. It is the word we find in Nehemiah, as the people gathered to hear God's word in a massive assembly (Nehemiah 8:8), and in Jesus' sermon in Nazareth, as he reads from Isaiah and explains it (Luke 4:16). Churches

---

17 R. Kent Hughes and Bryan Chappell, *1 & 2 Timothy and Titus* (Crossway, 2000), p 115.

today carry on this rich tradition as we read the Scriptures publicly and then hear them explained and applied in the assembly. God builds his people by his word. He sanctifies us through his truth (John 17:17). It is one of the primary ways in which we behold the glory of Christ and experience spiritual renewal (2 Corinthians 3:18 – 4:6).

So, listen to the sermon with a humble heart, expecting that God will change you through the preaching of his word. Paul Tripp states:

> *You cannot sit under the teaching of the word of God with an open and willing heart and remain the same. In teaching you, it recreates you in the likeness of the one who made you and gifted you ... The Bible is God's constant curriculum, and it has no graduation ceremony. No matter how long you have been a Christian, you will need its instruction today as much as you needed it on your first day as an infant Christian.*[18]

How we listen to the word matters! If we listen to the word humbly and eagerly, we will experience transformation (see Luke 8:9-15; James 1:21). We can experience that vivid image in the prophet Isaiah, where he says that Scripture is like the rain and snow that fall to the earth, and then says, "Instead of the thorn shall come up the cypress; instead the brier shall come up the myrtle" (Isaiah 55:13). In other words, radical transformation occurs.

---

18 Tripp, *Do You Believe?*, p 47.

HEARING GOD'S WORD: AN EXPOSITIONAL MOVEMENT

In Nehemiah 8, in the 5th century BC, God's people, having returned from the exile to Babylon, gather to celebrate the rebuilding of the walls of Jerusalem and to hear from his word. And here we find a remarkable story of what we would call today a "revival." At the center of it is an expositional movement.

While Ezra, the lead teacher, receives a lot of attention in the passage as the leader of a dramatic worship service, it is striking that the phrase "the people" appears 13 times in the chapter. We are being guided not to miss what the people of God are doing: gathering to hear the word of God. As we read through this chapter, we find the word being taught in a large setting (Nehemiah 8:1-6), then in smaller groups (v 7-8), and finally in homes (v 13-18). It is an inspiring vision of what we ideally see in church life today: the word preached in corporate worship; the word studied and applied in smaller settings; and the word taught and lived out in the home.

The people gathered that day were not worshiping Ezra—a reminder that, however great your preacher is, he is not to be placed on a pedestal; nor were they worshiping the Bible—a reminder that Bible knowledge itself is not the goal of gathering to hear the word preached. No—they were worshiping the God of the Bible, who has revealed himself in Holy Scripture: "And they told Ezra the scribe to bring the Book of the Law of Moses *that the Lord had commanded* Israel" (Nehemiah 8:1, my emphasis). As a result, they responded in ways that are often seen today only in acts of musical worship: saying "Amen," lifting up their hands, and bowing face down in worship (v 6-8). What was it that produced such a worshipful response?

First, they were "attentive" to the word (v 3). They were focused. If this were written today, the writer might say, "They were not looking at their smartphones!" They were hungry for the word.

Second, they were thinking hard. The writer places a strong emphasis on the need to "understand" the word. (v 2, 7, 8, 12). It was as God's people listened attentively to faithful teachers, and understood the message, that it changed them. This is a basic but important truth: for Scripture to change you, you need to understand it. The Bible is not a magic book, where, if we rub it the right way or sit in a room with it open at the front, it will change us. No, we become more like Jesus as we think— as we understand the word of Christ and allow it to have its transforming impact on us.

Third, as the scene unfolds in Nehemiah, the people are brought to the conviction of their sin (v 9-10), but the word then leads them to joy. Why? For one, there was the realization that God was not casting them off. He was merciful. Moreover, they were led to joy when they learned a bit more about God's grace and forgiveness. This first day of the seventh month (v 2) was a festival month that began with the Feast of Trumpets (see

Leviticus 23:23-25). This was a joyful time. Trumpets would be played, and the people would be reminded that on the 10th day of the month the greatest of all feasts was to occur: the Day of Atonement, when the high priest would take the blood of a sacrifice, walk into the Most Holy Place, and make atonement for the people he represented. In other words, they were told to celebrate because atonement was around the corner! And five days after the Day of Atonement, the Feast of Booths began, which reminded people of God's bountiful provision in the wilderness (Nehemiah 8:13-18; see Leviticus 23:33-36; Deuteronomy 16:15). This is why the leaders in the time of Ezra told the people to stop crying and start celebrating (Nehemiah 8:10)—not because sin should not make us weep but because the forgiveness of our sin should bring us through our tears to joy. "The joy of the Lord is our strength." (v 10).

It is the same for us today. As new-covenant believers, we have a greater atonement to rejoice in. The law makes us aware of our problem—sin—and we weep. But the gospel brings us the solution—Jesus—and we rejoice. The joy of Jesus our Redeemer is our strength. And that is why we should want to read the Bible and hear it proclaimed. The Bible tells the story of the true and better sacrifice. We love the Bible because the Bible is about the Messiah. We need the Bible because we do not know about the Savior without it. We can know about God generally in creation, but no one can get from sunsets to substitution, from fall leaves to forgiveness, apart from the Scriptures. We rejoice in the message of Scripture—or we might say, in the hero of Scripture—because through him our greatest problem has already been solved.

They say a picture is worth a thousand words, and I keep a picture in my office to remind me of the need of God's people for Christ-centered exposition. It is a picture of one of the many paintings of Lucas Cranach, the artist of the Reformation. It shows Martin Luther preaching at St. Mary's Church, Wittenberg, Germany (where he preached from 1514 onward).[19] The picture shows him with one finger on the text, and then with one finger pointing to Christ crucified. And the congregation's eyes are all fixed on Christ (not on their world-famous preacher!). That is the goal of preaching in the assembly. The rapper Tupac used to sing, "All eyes on me!" but at the heart of Christian preaching in corporate worship is another plea: "All eyes on Jesus." That is why preaching is a central part of our gathering. It is God's gift to you, to point you to his Son and your Savior week by week, reminding you by his Spirit of his love for you and changing you to become more like him. Remember that as the preacher gets into the pulpit next Sunday, and your view of what is happening over the next 40 (or 20 or 60!) minutes will be refreshed and transformed—and so will you.

---

19 See Andrew Pettegree, *Brand Luther* (Penguin, 2016), p 143-163.

ACTION STEPS

- *Prioritize the word read and preached.* Listen attentively and eagerly to the sermon, desiring to understand the message. Do not come as a sermon critic but as a hungry learner in need of gospel truth.

- *Listen to the sermon with your Bible open.* See where the points of the sermon are coming from. Consider how the Bible author says things. Commit texts of Scripture to memory as you hear them expounded.

- *Consider some practical ways to stay engaged in the sermon.* Consider taking notes, journaling, or responding verbally. Work at being an active listener.

- *Listen for the good of others.* What can you discuss later with your friend, roommate, spouse, kids, or small group?

- *Listen with a view to putting truth into practice.* This sometimes requires some thought after the sermon. That is fine. But do not merely listen for information; listen to apply.

- *Listen to worship.* Stay engaged to behold the wonder of Jesus revealed in Holy Scripture. Worship your way through the sermon.

4. GATHERING TO SING TOGETHER

Let the word of Christ dwell in you richly, teaching and admonishing one another in all wisdom, singing psalms and hymns and spiritual songs, with thankfulness in your hearts to God.
Colossians 3:16

One morning during corporate worship, I leaned toward one of the little girls in our church, Summer, who was trying to read the lyrics and sing along, and asked her, "Do you like church?" She replied, "Not really, but I like the singing." I appreciated her honesty!

A lot of Christians may agree with her. They really enjoy musical worship but do not care much for the other aspects of the gathering. On the other hand, a lot of Christians do not care for singing and would prefer not to have to do it. I recall talking to a friend about a church he was attending, and he told me, "Yeah, I don't like the music at all, but I enjoy the preaching. That's why I like to arrive 10 to 15 minutes late." I tried to persuade him to rethink this practice.

In a sense, our culture does not help us with our singing in the gathering because we live in a world of concerts, where we go to watch a performance and enjoy the atmosphere but are not in any way central or essential to what is going on.

What are we to make of all these ideas? Why do we sing together, and does it really matter? A brief survey of Scripture reveals a number of reasons why, and how, Christians sing.[20]

GOD'S WORD TELLS US TO SING, AND OUR SINGING ENCOURAGES OTHERS

The Bible is filled with commands to praise the Lord. You only need to open the Psalms and read them! The Psalms have been called the "hymn book of the Bible" or the "prayer book of the Bible," and they provide us with a rich source of praise, prayer and lament in worship. Over and over, we are told to praise God (for example, Psalms 146 – 150). The psalmists tell us that it is good and fitting to sing to God (see Psalm 92:1; 147:1). And in commanding us to praise him, as C.S. Lewis pointed out, God is also inviting us to enjoy him.[21] Here, then, are our first two reasons why singing matters when we gather:

---

20 A whole lot more could be said about singing, like creation and the heavenly host singing. For instance, there was singing at creation, "when the morning stars sang together and all the sons of God shouted for joy" (Job 38:7); but it is not my purpose to address these matters.

21 C.S. Lewis, "Reflections on the Psalms," *The Inspirational Writings of C.S. Lewis* (Inspirational Press, 1994), p 179-80.

first, we're commanded to sing; second, we'll enjoy the Lord as we do so.

Two particular texts on singing in the New Testament really stand out. Both highlight not only the admonition to sing but also emphasize how our singing instructs and encourages other believers:

Let the word of Christ dwell in you richly, teaching and admonishing one another in all wisdom, singing psalms and hymns and spiritual songs, with thankfulness in your hearts to God. (Colossians 3:16)

And do not get drunk with wine, for that is debauchery, but be filled with the Spirit, addressing one another in psalms and hymns and spiritual songs, singing and making melody to the Lord with your heart, giving thanks always and for everything to God the Father in the name of our Lord Jesus Christ. (Ephesians 5:18-20)

Spirit-filled, word-saturated believers are called on to sing a variety of songs, to the Lord and to one another.[22]

So the third reason to sing is this: our singing can contribute to the encouragement and well-being of others. As a new Christian I never really thought about how my singing could encourage someone else, but that is what Paul says it does. In our time, it has been very common to have this "me and Jesus" feel in worship

---

22 Often people try to differentiate between three types of songs here, but I think that a rigid distinction is unnecessary. In both Psalm 66:1 and 75:1, for instance, two terms are used in the superscriptions to describe one psalm.

services. The lights over the congregation are down, the lights on the stage up, and no one can see anyone in the room. But that is not what Paul is thinking of and exhorting us to do. It seems best for lights to be up so that you can see your Bible and so that you can see your fellow church members as you sing with and to them, for the purpose of encouraging them.

You may be thinking, "Yeah, but I'm not a singer." I can identify with that problem! Thankfully we can "make melody to the Lord in our hearts" (Ephesians 5:19). God hears what no one else hears, and a believer who pours out his or her heart in praise glorifies God. Singing is more about our hearts than our voices. And our singing—whether or not we are in tune—can strengthen a weaker brother or sister who is struggling. The voice of God's people has a powerful way of encouraging others.

Singing, then, is for every believer, not just for those with good voices or who are trained musicians (as thankful as we are for such individuals!). It's a gift to our own hearts, and it's our gift to others in the gathering. Our aim should not be to produce a concert but rather a group of family members singing cherished songs with their arms around each other, or the feel of old friends at the pub singing local songs that they grew up with, or Boston Red Sox fans every eighth inning or England soccer fans before and after a game singing "Sweet Caroline" at the top of their lungs. We do not gather to watch the gifted, but we gather to participate as members of the body. As our worship pastor often says, "The most important sound in corporate worship is the congregation."

OUR SINGING REFLECTS GOD'S CHARACTER

Did you know that God sings about you? The psalmists say that he delights in his people (Psalm 35:27; 149:4). And the prophet Zephaniah gives us what John Piper calls an "almost unbelievable promise":[23]

The LORD your God is in your midst,
  a mighty one who will save;
he will rejoice over you with gladness;
  he will quiet you by his love;
he will exult over you with loud singing.

(Zephaniah 3:17)

What a picture! God is present with his people and singing loudly over them with gladness and love. The mighty God who saves is the God who also sings. If you are in Christ, the Father sings over you—loudly and gladly and lovingly, and you can return his song in your worship—loudly, gladly, and lovingly!

Not only do we see God the Father singing but God the Son, too. We read of our Savior singing hymns with his disciples on the night before his death at Golgotha (Matthew 26:30). Jesus obviously thought singing was significant and meaningful. We find him reflecting on Psalm 22 on the cross (Matthew 27:46). He died with

---

23 John Piper, *The Pleasures of God*, Revised Edition (Multnomah, 2015), p 178.

the psalms on his lips. In his commentary on the Psalms, Christopher Ash points out that Jesus is the great singer of the Psalms, and that as we read or sing them, we can hear his voice as that of the Messiah praying, lamenting, teaching, and praising.[24] To immerse ourselves in the Psalms and to sing hymns to God is to follow Jesus and be conformed into his likeness.

Unsurprisingly, therefore, we find God's people singing throughout history. After the Israelites are freed from Egypt and cross the Red Sea, they sing to the Lord (Exodus 15:1-21). This is often understood as the first song in the Bible. Apparently, Moses penned it right after the deliverance. The liberated people sing to the Lord and about the Lord—about his character and his works.

The New Testament gives us passages that contain heightened poetic language, packed with doctrine, about the person and work of Christ, which may have been parts of early creeds or songs (for example, Philippians 2:6-11; Colossians 1:15-20; 1 Timothy 2:5-6; 3:16; 2 Timothy 2:11-13; Hebrews 1:1-4). This pattern of praise continues throughout the biblical narrative until we get to the last book of the Bible, where we read of various songs of praise, as in Revelation 5, where worship is given to the Lamb, who redeemed his people with his blood (v 9). And in heaven, the song of Exodus 15 is still

---

24 Christopher Ash, *Teaching Psalms* (Christian Focus, 2017), p 38.

being sung, for God has not changed: John calls it, "The Song of Moses and of the Lamb" (Revelation 15:3).

So, singing with the congregation is more than "mood music." We are aligning ourselves with the people of God throughout history, who have joyfully, reverently, gratefully, and humbly sung praises to God. We sing in good times and bad; when we're high and when we're low; when we feel like it and when we do not. We sing because our hearts are joyful, and we sing in order to encourage our hearts to become joyful. We sing knowing that soon all of our pain and grief will give way to eternal glory (Romans 8:18-31). We sing to remember where our true citizenship lies (Philippians 3:20-21; Hebrews 13:14-15).

HOW CAN WE *NOT* SING?

The Gospel of Luke opens with exuberant joy and praise. Mary's song is the first of four songs of the incarnation (Luke 1:46-55), and it begins with exultant praise: "My soul magnifies the Lord, and my spirit rejoices in God my Savior" (v 46-47). Her song is followed by Zechariah's song of salvation (v 68-79). Next, we read of the angels giving glory to God (2:14). Finally, we read of Simeon's song (v 29-32). But others are praising God too, including Anna (v 36-38) and the shepherds (v 20). Some have called Luke the church's first hymnologist.

It is significant that if you look at the songs of Mary and Zechariah in Luke 1, you can actually cut them out altogether and not lose anything in the narrative. So why does Luke include these songs? I think he is showing us *how we should respond to the good news: in singing of our love for and adoration of God.*

Mary's worship is instructive for us today, in at least four ways. First, her worship is wholehearted and joy-filled— "my spirit," she says, *"rejoices* in God my Savior" (v 46, my emphasis). She worships with all that she is. And she shows us the secret to joy: magnify God. Our culture today tells us, "To maximize joy you need to minimize God." But Mary's song reveals the real truth: to maximize joy you need to *magnify* God.

Second, her worship is *personal.* She speaks of "my Savior." The message of the gospel is historical and theological, but it is also intensely personal.

Third, her worship is *God-centered* ("magnifies the *Lord"* and "*God* my Savior"). She goes on in the song to praise God for his attributes and his actions: for who he is and what he has done and all that he will do. I have often tried to think about Mary's context and get a sense of what she felt like in this moment. She had a lot to worry about. But her worry gives way to worship when she contemplates the being of God. Our songs, when filled with good theology, also help to settle us and enliven us.

Fourth, her worship is *Bible-saturated.* Many people don't think Mary could have written this because she was so young, and it is so majestic and so theological. So where did she get all this depth? Simple: Mary knew her Bible! The song is loaded with Old Testament allusions and phrases. There are echoes of Genesis, Deuteronomy, 1 and 2 Samuel, Job, Psalms, Isaiah, Ezekiel, Micah, Habakkuk, and Zephaniah, and more.

We know the same God as Mary and trust the same gospel as she did. We will surely, therefore, sing as she did. So, next time you are in the gathering, sing. Sing with your heart, not just your lips. Think about the gospel truths in the lyrics, and let those flood and thrill your heart. Encourage your own soul and the souls of your brothers and sisters. Be sure that if a non-Christian came to your church for the first time and saw you singing, they would think, "They clearly believe what they are singing. I'd better take this gospel message seriously too."

ACTION STEPS

How should we approach the singing portion of our gatherings?

- *Recognize that this is something that we can all do.* Whether or not you love to sing outside the gathering and whether or not you are good at singing, you are still commanded to sing. So, do!

- *Remember that you can encourage your brothers and sisters through your singing.* We sing both to the Lord and to one another. One of the sisters in our church was grieving the loss of a loved one recently and told our worship pastor, "I just don't think I can sing today." He responded, "Then allow the songs of your brothers and sisters to encourage you."

- *Remember that when we gather to sing, we join with a great history of saints who have sung God's praise, and one day we will do it in the new creation.* This gives us a sense of wonder and dignity. This is our heritage, and this is where history is going!

- *Sing prayerfully.* As you hear the gospel sung, pray for others to hear the message and be changed. As you hear bold declarations made in song, pray that God would grant you grace to obey.

5. GATHERING TO PRAY TOGETHER

First of all, then, I urge that supplications, prayers, intercessions, and thanksgivings be made for all people, for kings and all who are in high positions, that we may lead a peaceful and quiet life, godly and dignified in every way.
1 Timothy 2:1-2

Here is the claim of this chapter: *prayer is a gift, and praying with other believers is a double gift.* We have the privilege of calling out to God together because of the transforming impact of the gospel in our lives. Paul gives us this foundational text on prayer: "For through him [Jesus] we both [Jew and Gentile] have access in one Spirit to the Father" (Ephesians 2:18).

However, corporate prayer seems to be minimized today. When there is a focus on prayer, it is usually on individual prayer. As important as this is (Matthew 6:5-6), we need to also see how vitally important—how biblical—corporate prayer is.

PRAYING TOGETHER IN THE BIBLE

Examples of prayer for the people of God by the people of God abound in the Old Testament.[25] In slavery in Egypt, the people cry out to God together when in bondage to Egypt (Exodus 2:23). In the book of Judges, God's people cry for deliverance frequently (Judges 3:9, 15; 4:3; 6:6-7). During David's reign, we have a golden era of corporate prayer, given the number of psalms that bear his name and that encourage the people to pour out their hearts to God (Psalm 52), as they call on God to "remember his congregation" (Psalm 74), as the people are exhorted to give thanks to God (Psalm 75), as they ask God to revive his people (Psalm 85), as they ask God to help them (Psalm 108), and as they express their hope for redemption (Psalm 130).

Later writings in Old Testament history bring us more corporate petitions, led by individuals such as Nehemiah (Nehemiah 1:4-11). We read, too, of corporate repentance (Ezra 10) and corporate confession (Nehemiah 9:1-38).

In the New Testament, we should begin by noting that the "Lord's Prayer" has a corporate emphasis: "*Our* Father... give *us* ... forgive *us* ... lead *us* ... deliver *us*" (Matthew 6:9-13). Further, Jesus' prayer on the night before he died emphasized his desire for unity: "... that

---

25 I'm indebted to Jim Hamilton for bringing to mind many of these references. See "A Biblical Theology for Corporate Prayer," https://www.9marks.org/article/biblical-theology-corporate-prayer/ (accessed Dec. 30, 2021).

they may all be one, just as you, Father, are in me, and I in you, that they also may be in us, so that the world may believe that you have sent me" (John 17:21).

The book of Acts is, in terms of its frequent corporate prayers, the New Testament equivalent of Psalms, for it records numerous instances of prayer from beginning to end (many of them using the Psalms as their basis—for instance, Acts 4:23-31). It is worth listing them because we can see vivid examples of the church in prayer, and these can give us some ideas of what we might pray about:

- The disciples pray when seeking Judas' replacement (1:12-26).

- The church is "devoted to prayer" when they assemble (2:42).

- The church prays for boldness when facing opposition (4:23-31).

- The church prays for selected leaders, and leaders express their commitment to prayer (6:1-6).

- Stephen, the first martyr, prays for the forgiveness of those putting him to death (7:59-60).

- Peter and John pray for the Samaritans, that they may receive the Holy Spirit (8:14-15).

- The Gentile Cornelius and the apostle Peter are brought together in the context of prayer (Acts 10 – 11).

- The church prays for Peter's release from prison (12:1-5), and when Peter is delivered, he returns to find the church holding a prayer meeting (12:12).

- The church in Antioch fasts and prays before sending out Paul and Barnabas on mission (13:1-3).

- After appointing elders in new churches, Paul and Barnabas pray for the elders and commit them to the Lord (14:2-3).

- After seeing conversions in Philippi, Paul and Barnabas are put in prison, where, Luke says, they were "praying and singing hymns to God" (16:25).

- Before leaving Ephesus, Paul prays for the elders (20:36).[26]

Notice how frequently believers were praying with other believers! The church practiced both free and formal times of prayer. They prayed in all sorts of contexts—in the temple, in homes, along the road, when encountering the sick and afflicted, before preaching, or when persecuted.

---

26 This list is adapted from John Onwuchekwa, *Prayer: How Praying Together Shapes the Church* (Crossway, 2018), p 94-95.

They prayed over particular situations. Luke gives us a picture of the early church as being made up of those with limited earthly resources but who had the necessary power to shake the world, and this came through prayer.

In the epistles, we read a host of exhortations to pray and instructions about prayer.[27] Paul asks the church for prayer for his own ministry.[28] He includes many prayers for the believers in his epistles.[29] The apostle also states that corporate prayer has the purpose of building up the church (1 Corinthians 14:16-17). He tells Timothy to lead the church in prayer for those in leadership, and instructs men to be known for prayer and not quarreling (1 Timothy 2:1-2, 8).

Corporate prayer is a heavenly, as well as an earthly, reality. Revelation takes us to heavenly realities and shows us that martyrs who have gone before us are asking the Father to avenge their blood (Revelation 6:9-11). The prayers of the saints are like incense before the throne (8:1-4). And the final verse of the Bible ends with a prayer: "Amen. Come, Lord Jesus!" (22:20).

The Bible, then, is filled with examples of corporate prayer—praying together with and praying on behalf of

---

27 Romans 12:12; Philippians 4:6-7; Colossians 4:2; 1 Thessalonians 5:16-18; James 5:13-18; 1 Peter 3:7; 4:7; Jude 20.

28 Romans 15:30; 2 Corinthians 1:11; Ephesians 6:19; Philippians 1:19; Colossians 4:3 – 4; 1 Thessalonians 5:25.

29 Ephesians 1:15-23; 3:14-21; Philippians 1:3-5; Colossians 1:9-12; 1 Thessalonians 1:2-3.

the people of God. We must not view as supplemental or optional what the early church viewed as essential. When we assemble together in our churches, corporate prayer should be at the heart of what we do, not treated as an add-on or a transitional moment. Then we will be carrying on this great heritage of God's people calling out to God in prayer for their good and for the glory of his name.

THE BENEFITS OF CORPORATE PRAYER

Space does not permit us to consider all the benefits of corporate prayer, but allow me to note four of them.

First, corporate prayer, when reflecting on the truth of the gospel, *recenters us on the good news*. During the week our hearts and minds can be all over the place. We can easily drift into thinking of all kinds of untrue and impure things. But when someone leads a group of people in praying together—mourning over the suffering of this present age but also rejoicing in the glory that will be revealed, which is made possible through the atoning work of Christ for sinners like us—such a prayer has a transforming effect. All of our problems get put into their proper place when we recognize afresh that through the crucified and risen Christ, our greatest problem has already been solved.

Second, prayer in church *reminds us of our unity in the faith*. Christian unity is not something we create; only Jesus does that, by he work of his Spirit. But unity is something that we must seek to *maintain* (Ephesians 4:1-6). One of the ways in which we maintain unity is through times of corporate prayer. During these times of prayer, we grow together as we reflect on our new identity as children of God. We grow together as we pray for common goals, for one another, for the pastors' leadership, for those hurting in the church, for those in need of provision, and for those who are sick. We grow together as we confess the sins that divide us and as we pray for God to reconcile us to one another. Our unity is strengthened as we rejoice with those who rejoice and weep with those who weep (Romans 12:15). We grow stronger as we pray when persecuted or when we have big evangelistic opportunities in front of us. Few things are more beautiful or encouraging than seeing a group of Christians gathered before the throne of grace, lifting up their prayers to God.

Third, corporate prayer, when rightly prioritized, has the power to bring *spiritual renewal to the church*. Throughout the Bible, we see God answering the prayers of his people. We see it in church history, too, as we read of revivals happening and of people being converted when corporate prayer is prioritized. Consider the first Great Awakening (which peaked between 1740 and 1742). It was preceded by a long period of persecution in Britain. In his biography of George Whitefield, Arnold Dallimore makes a link between the prayers of the saints in prison and the revivals that followed:

> *Legislation was enacted which distressed the Puritan*
> *conscience, and in 1662, on one of the darkest days in*
> *all British history, nearly two thousand ministers—*
> *all those who would not submit to the Act of*
> *Uniformity—were ejected from their livings. Hundreds*
> *of these men suffered throughout the rest of their*
> *lives, and a number died in prison. Yet these terrible*
> *conditions became the occasion of a great volume of*
> *prayer; forbidden to preach under threat of severe*
> *penalties—as John Bunyan's Bedford imprisonment*
> *bore witness—they yet could pray, and only eternity*
> *will reveal the relationship between this burden of*
> *supplication and the revival that followed.*[30]

We need to pray together because we want to see God renew and revive his church.

Prayer is often the means God uses to free us and our brothers and sisters from dark spiritual attacks. How should we help those who are in bondage to various sins or have grown bitter, afraid, cold, anxious, or depressed? By seeking God together on their behalf for their own spiritual renewal and growth. We must wage war in this spiritual battle with the weapon of prayer.

For, by God's grace, our prayers make a difference. Spurgeon told his congregation:

---

30 Arnold Dallimore, *George Whitefield*, Vol. 1 (The Banner of Truth Trust, 2001), p 19–20.

As many mercies are conveyed from Heaven in the ship of prayer, so there are many choice and special favors which can only be brought to us by the fleets of united prayer. Many are the good things which God will give to His lonely Elijahs and Daniels, but if two of you agree as touching anything that you shall ask, there is no limit to God's bountiful answers. Peter might never have been brought out of prison if it had not been that prayer was made without ceasing by all the Church for him. Pentecost might never have come if all the disciples had not been, "with one accord in one place," waiting for the descent of the tongues of fire. God is pleased to give many mercies to one pleader, but at times He seems to say, "You shall all appear before Me and entreat My favor, for I will not see your face, unless even your Brothers and Sisters are with you."[31]

Fourth and finally, prayer gives everyone *an opportunity to engage in mission*. It is right to think of prayer being preparation for our mission, but it is also central to the work of mission. Consider how the apostle Paul requested prayer for his ministry (Colossians 4:2-3; Ephesians 6:18-20). So all Christians today also have the opportunity of engaging in mission by lifting up faithful gospel servants.

What a privilege to seek God together with our brothers and sisters, and what power there is in that.

---

31 Charles Spurgeon, "The Power of Prayer and the Pleasure of Praise," https://ccel. org/ccel/spurgeon/sermons09/sermons09.xxi.html (accessed Dec. 30, 2021).

Remembering this will prevent you from seeing prayer in your gatherings as less dynamic than singing or preaching, and from carelessly adding your amen at the end of the prayers without focusing or thinking during the prayers. For praying in the gathering is not something you are called to watch but something you are called to do.

In his excellent book on prayer, pastor John Onwuchekwa reminds us that we are participants, not season-ticket holders:

> I thought I hated baseball. I watched it to cure insomnia. Then one day in elementary school, my friends came to the door with aluminum baseball bats and tennis balls. We used cars and lampposts in our cul-de-sac as bases, and we started playing baseball. And you know what? Baseball wasn't that bad. In fact, baseball was great! It was suddenly engaging and enjoyable. We played for hours, and the time just flew. It wasn't baseball I hated. It was just watching it. What made the difference? Participation. The worth of the sport shouldn't be judged by spectating but by participating.[32]

Whether or not you share Onwuchekwa's view of watching baseball, his point is worth noting. Might it be that many of us do not value corporate prayer because we have not found ways to meaningfully engage in

---

32 Onwuchekwa, *Prayer*, p 77.

prayer with others? Might the time fly by once we do? How will you pick up the ball and bat, so to speak, and start participating?

ACTION STEPS

- *When someone is leading in corporate prayer, pray along with them.* I usually lead the pastoral prayer time at our church, and by this I mean an extended time of thanksgiving and intercession. Prior to voicing this prayer, I often say something like this: "I'm going to pray now, but I want you to pray with me." Some of the sweetest sounds on Sunday morning are when I hear people giving audible expressions to these petitions, like "Yes, Lord," "Amen," "Please, Lord," and "Thank you, Lord."

- *Be ruthless with worldly tangents (where your mind drifts to thinking of work, or chores, or whatever)—notice them and actively draw your mind back from them. Equally, though, be prayerful in godly tangents (where your mind considers people who are in a time of trial, or a nation where the church is persecuted, or an area of your life where you need help to change or obey God) and pray for those people or areas the Spirit has drawn you to speak to God about.*

- *Pray with others after the service—when you finish a conversation, pause to pray together.*

- *Ask for prayer*. It's humbling. But it's deeply encouraging.

- *If you have an opportunity to lead corporate prayer, or to pray in a small group or just with a friend, aim to use the Bible.* Learn to pray about the priorities of Scripture and to pray the promises of God back to him. The issues that are most emphasized in the Bible are spiritual issues rather than material needs, and so that should direct our prayers; and we should remember that God's promises invite us to pray for what he promises (see 1 Kings 18; Daniel 9:2 with Jeremiah 29:10-14; Revelation 22:20). Offer prayers of praise, of confession, of intercession, and of thanksgiving.

6. CELEBRATE THE GOSPEL VISUALLY

The Lord Jesus on the night when he was betrayed
took bread, and when he had given thanks, he broke it,
and said, "This is my body, which is for you. Do this in
remembrance of me."
1 Corinthians 11:23-24

"**W**hat did you like about worship?" This was often the starter question on the ride home from church when my kids were younger. My youngest, Joshua, would regularly answer by focusing on the Lord's Supper. It clearly left an impression on him. He almost never talked about my sermon, but he did talk about the Table.

Why? The Lord's Supper (or Communion, the Eucharist, or the Table) gives us a picture of the gospel. Joshua was not able to articulate the great doctrines of the faith, but he could see the good news as the bread was torn and the fruit of the vine poured out. Every week he was able to reflect on Jesus' death for sinners—on the Lamb that was slain for the world.

The other "ordinance" of the church, baptism, was not something the kids witnessed every week, but when they did, it invariably became the main thing they talked about. Baptism also pictures the gospel. It is an amazing testimony of the transforming grace of God and the believer's union with Christ.

There are various ways God has given us to help us rejoice in the gospel and reflect on its vast implications, and two are the ordinances given to us by the Lord Jesus, practiced by the early church, and carried on to this day: baptism and Communion.

Throughout history, various aspects of these practices have been hotly debated, and I am not going to answer every question about them. I simply want to describe some of the reasons why they are significant for us as we gather today.

RECAPTURING THE AWE

I imagine some readers—perhaps including you—are tempted to skip a chapter about baptism and the Lord's Supper. There are a number of reasons why we may have a low view of the ordinances, especially the Lord's Supper, including: (1) a bad church experience in the past; (2) the desire to keep church from feeling "too churchy"; (3) the feeling that the ordinances interrupt the "flow of worship"; (4) the notion that these practices are "mere symbols" and thus carry little real significance; or (5) the fact that we are so familiar with them that they no longer bring a sense of expectancy and joy. Much could be said about these, but (1) a bad experience of something good does not make the good thing itself a bad thing, to be avoided or downplayed; (2) if Jesus commands something, his people need to obey, and if the Jesus who loves us enough to lay down his life for us commands something, we can trust that he commands it for our good; (3) since true worship is always based on God's commands, offering to him what pleases him, we should steer clear of allowing feelings-based considerations to trump Scriptural guidance or commands. With that said, let's focus more on reasons 4 and 5.

Reason 4: These holy ordinances are more than symbols. New Testament scholar Ray Van Neste says, "We ought never speak like the pastor who regularly admonished his congregation upon observing the Supper: 'Now, remember that this doesn't mean anything. These are just symbols.'"[33] Because some well-intended church leaders want to avoid teaching anything "magical" when it comes to Communion and to avoid all the erroneous teaching about it, they can easily gravitate to another problem: namely, conveying a low view of the Table. Such a negative view of the Lord's Supper negates any sense of awed delight in partaking in it and suggests that we should not to expect anything special to occur during Communion.

---

33 Ray Van Neste, "The Lord's Supper in the Context of the Local Church," *The Lord's Supper* (B&H, 2010), p 365.

Yes, there are many misunderstandings of Communion. But we should not let abuses of it keep us from experiencing the blessing of the Table, where we enjoy sweet communion with Christ, we express our unity as the family of God, and we participate in this sign of the messianic reign of Christ.

Reason 5: Regarding *familiarity*, remember that this problem is not limited to the Lord's Supper. I have heard people objecting to frequently taking the Lord's Supper on the basis that it will get over-familiar and stop seeming significant. But almost no one says this about preaching or singing! The problem is not with the frequency but with our hearts. We are in a spiritually dangerous place when we get familiar with the means that God has given us for our growth as disciples. But it can happen. So the question should be: *how can we recapture the awe?*

A COMMITMENT AND A COMMAND

One way to overcome these problems is by reflecting on terminology. Baptism and the Lord's Supper have been called various things, but one broadly used term throughout church history has been "sacraments."

The term "sacrament" is derived from the Latin word *sacramentum*, which originally referred to an oath of loyalty made by a soldier to his commander. The word "sacrament" therefore became an apt way for the early church to express the nature of the Lord's Supper and of baptism. Both are outward signs expressing inward grace and faith-filled commitment to the Lord.[34]

As time went on, however, the church adopted a view that went beyond this basic understanding, believing that the sacraments themselves were able to infuse the grace of God into the individual in an almost mechanical way, regardless of that person's spiritual condition (that is, whether they had faith or not). During the Reformation in the early 1500s, this was called into question, as Martin Luther and others argued from Scripture that we receive God's saving grace by faith alone.

Protestants today often use the word "sacrament" without the idea that it automatically conveys grace apart from faith. We may use it in a very *general* sense, a sacrament simply being a rite or ceremony instituted by Jesus. Or we may refer to baptism and the Lord's Supper as sacraments in the sense of involving *vows of loyalty and commitment to Christ*. When used in these ways, the term "sacrament" becomes legitimate and meaningful. Baptism gives the believer the opportunity to *first* affirm their loyalty to Christ, and the Lord's Supper gives the believer the opportunity to *repeatedly* affirm their loyalty to Christ.[35]

Expressing our loyalty to Jesus in ways that he mandated is a big deal. We should ponder these sacraments with

---

34 Stanley J. Grenz, *The Baptist Congregation* (Regent College Publishing, 1985), p 29.

35 Grenz, p 31.

the gravity of a soldier committing himself or herself to their commander to be faithful unto death. In fact, in parts of the world hostile to Christianity, a believer's baptism may get him or her killed, or at least alienated from their own family. It is easy in less hostile contexts to view baptism as being sentimental and heart-warming, but not something that is particularly serious. But if we really ponder the depth of such a declaration—that "Jesus is Lord, and I will follow him unto death"—it has the power to wake us up, reminding us of what matters in life, of the cost of following Jesus, of the certainty of death, and of the glory that we will enjoy eternally.

Others prefer to use the term "ordinance," which is derived from the word "ordain."[36] Why is this significant? Because it communicates that *Jesus himself ordained these practices for his followers, and they should thus be highly prized in our hearts*. We should not view something that Jesus mandated as being trivial. The Gospel of Luke contains Jesus' words about the Lord's Supper in reference to his upcoming crucifixion:

And he took bread, and when he had given thanks, he broke it and gave it to them, saying, "This is my body, which is given for you. Do this in remembrance of me." And likewise the cup after they had eaten, saying, "This cup that is poured out for you is the new covenant in my blood." (Luke 22:19-20)

---

36 Grenz, p 30.

And the Gospel of Matthew contains the command of Christ regarding baptism. After his resurrection...

Jesus came and said to them, "All authority in heaven and on earth has been given to me. Go therefore and make disciples of all nations, baptizing them in the name of the Father and of the Son and of the Holy Spirit, teaching them to observe all that I have commanded you. And behold, I am with you always, to the end of the age." (Matthew 28:18-20)

When we practice these ordinances, we are following the commands of Jesus, the Savior who died for us, rose for us, and will return for us.

The significance of these ordinances is highlighted when we simply ask the question, "What makes a true church?" It is not a building, bylaws, a bulletin, or a band! The widely held historical position has been that a true church exists when the gospel is preached and the sacraments are administered.[37] (Implied in this second mark was also the belief in the necessity of church discipline.) So whether you call them ordinances, sacraments, or something else, be sure to value them because they lie at the heart of what makes your church a church, rather than merely a Christian concert or a speaking venue.

---

37 See Mark Dever, *Nine Marks of a Healthy Church* (Crossway, 2000), p 8-9.

REMEMBER YOUR IDENTITY

I pastor a "credo-baptist" church, which baptizes those who are professing faith for themselves (rather than a "paedo-baptist" church, which baptizes the children of professing Christians—both views are based on the Bible and held by Christians who are thoughtfully and humbly seeking to follow Scripture). As a Baptist church, some of the most memorable days in the our life together have been when people have been baptized on Sundays. It is thrilling to hear new converts read their testimonies to the congregation, declaring Jesus as Lord, and then watch them being immersed in water as a visible display of their union with Christ in his death and resurrection (Romans 6:3-4), of the forgiveness of sins, and of their calling to walk in new life by the power of the Spirit. These moments are so powerful in their presentation of the gospel that I often say afterwards that I now don't need to preach a sermon (though I still do, of course!)

We have done these baptisms in various places: in a portable baptistery at a storefront, at a lake, and now in a built-in baptistery in our current church building. Regardless of the location, joy and praise have characterized those moments. The baptized person is proclaiming to the world, "I'm with Jesus. He is my Lord. I am new in him." But not only that—they are also saying, "I'm with Jesus' people. I am united to my fellow believers, as brothers and sisters." And they are making a proclamation to the spiritual realm, declaring that the risen Jesus Christ is Lord and that one day he will reign, putting all his enemies under his feet.[38]

What should you do as you observe someone making such a powerful visible declaration of their new identity? One thing is to *remember your baptism* (or, if you cannot remember it, then remember your moment or time of personal commitment)—remember who you are in Christ. Scholar Kevin Vanhoozer offers this compelling word:

[Baptism] is also an object lesson, a visual demonstration of a doctrinal truth concerning union with Christ. Water baptism inserts the disciple, in a very visible and tangible manner, into the story of Jesus. Baptism marks a disciple's setting out on Jesus' way by ritually enacting the death of the old self and the birth of the new ... It is a communicative act that corresponds to the disciple's new reality in Christ ... It is a rich theological lesson that also grips the church's imagination, particularly when congregants are exhorted to "remember your baptism" as they watch the baptism of someone else.[39]

Gathering with God's people to watch a new brother or sister be baptized is significant not just because you want to encourage them in the faith but because it is a powerful way to remember all that by faith is true of you,

---

38 Tony Merida, *Exalting Jesus in Romans* (B&H, 2021), p 96-106.

39 Kevin Vanhoozer, *Hearers and Doers* (Lexham, 2019), p 151.

so that you are excited and awed all over again at what Jesus Christ has done, is doing, and will do for you.

REMEMBER YOUR HOPE

Jesus explained the meaning of his death at a meal, and gave us that meal to remember his death (Mark 14:22-25). At the Passover meal, Jesus took the position of the host and used the bread and wine not to recall (as had been done for centuries) how God rescued his people from slavery in Egypt but to explain that now, through his death, God would rescue his people from sin and judgment. And he told his disciples to remember his death by continuing this holy ordinance until they would eat and drink once more with him in the kingdom (Luke 22:14-23).

This meal has many names, such as the *Eucharist* (from the Greek word for to "give thanks"), *Communion* (emphasizing the fellowship we have with the Lord), or the *Lord's Supper* (which finds its source in the link between the ordinance and the meals which Jesus shared with others, especially the final Passover meal he had with his disciples the night before his crucifixion).[40] Each term speaks to the meal's significance. We take it with Christ-honoring *thankfulness* in our hearts, with love for the Christ who *communes* with his people, and with awe and praise, knowing that God's people, the church, through the ages have enjoyed the Table together, proclaiming Jesus' death until he comes (see Acts 2:42-47; 1 Corinthians 11:17-34).

---

40 Grenz, *The Baptist Congregation*, p 39.

Meals can be powerful. Think for a moment of your favorite meal. You have probably picked one that not only had wonderful cuisine but included wonderful company or where something particularly significant happened—a night you did not want to end. At the same time, we also know the pain of losing someone and feeling their absence at the dinner table. These experiences are communicating something to us: we are made for the Table. We are made for the future experience of glory described by Isaiah (Isaiah 25:6-8)—for the marriage supper of the Lamb described by John (Revelation 19:6-10). The Lord's Supper reminds us of where history is heading for all those who trust Jesus: a wonderful feast in the presence of Jesus and his people.

The Lord's Supper, like some of our favorite childhood meals, has the power to remind us of home. It is saying to you, in tangible form, *In this life you will have trouble* (John 16:33), *but one day you will dine in your true home with the King.* We all need this hope. We all face pain, grief, loss, tears, sickness, disappointment, discouragement, anxiety, and conflict. But soon we will be brought into the new heaven and the new earth, and we will rejoice with God's people in the presence of the Lamb, who was slain for us. Then we will feel more at home than we have ever felt in our lives. The Lord's Supper helps us to taste and see this hope. It helps us taste the forgiveness that Jesus has brought us through his atoning death— the forgiveness is real as much as the Table is real bread and wine. It helps us see what it cost him to provide our salvation—it was a real sacrifice. It helps us imagine what it will be like when we see our King and sit at the Table anew in the kingdom—there is a real kingdom to come.

So when next your church is celebrating a baptism or the Lord's Supper, let it speak to you as Christ intended. Let it move your heart to awe and gratitude for his gospel. Jesus gave these ordinances as a kindness to us, to picture the gospel that saves us.

ACTION STEPS

- *If you are a believer and have not been baptized, let me encourage you to speak with a pastor.* Isn't it time for you to publicly confess that Jesus is your Lord in the presence of other believers?

- *Do you know someone who claims to be a Christian but has not been baptized?* Let me encourage you to discuss this issue with them. Show them the significance of baptism from the Scriptures and walk with them through this process. Perhaps set up a meeting with a pastor.

- *When you are observing a baptism, remember yours.* Remember that God brought you from death to life, that your sins have been forgiven, that the Spirit indwells you, and that you will one day experience a bodily resurrection because you are united to the risen Christ.

- *When you prepare for the Lord's Supper, take time to repent, reflect, and rejoice.* Communion is a time of self-examination (1 Corinthians 11:28). Approach the Table with a sense of repentance coupled with confidence that you are coming to our sympathetic high priest, who gives grace and mercy in our time of need (Hebrews 4:14-16). What is called for is not moral perfection but Christ-centered repentance. He invites imperfect, forgiven people to dine with him.

- *When you take the Lord's Supper, consider the unity that you share with other believers.* The Table illustrates our oneness in Christ. We all come as sinners to the same Savior, sharing the same hope.

- *Long to see more people baptized and take the bread and cup with you.* Allow these practices to stir up evangelistic zeal for your unbelieving friends, family, and neighbors.

7. GATHERING TO REACH OUTSIDERS

By this all people will know that you are my disciples, if you have love for one another.
John 13:35

Those who have been saved by grace should be known for graciously welcoming outsiders into their gatherings.

Sadly, that does not always happen. In his autobiography, Mahatma Gandhi wrote that during his student days, he read the Gospels seriously and considered becoming a Christian. He believed that in the teachings of Jesus he could find the solution to the caste system that was dividing the people of India. So one Sunday he decided to attend services at a nearby church and talk to the minister about becoming a Christian. However, when he entered the building, the usher refused to give him a seat and suggested that he go worship with his own people. Gandhi left the church and never returned. He wrote:

If Christians have caste differences also, I might as well remain a Hindu.[41]

You will (I hope) be certain that you and your church would not treat anyone this way. But it is possible to do the same thing in less obvious ways. Too many non-Christians have stories to tell of trying church and being made to feel unwelcome because of their appearance (race, hairstyle, dress, piercings, tattoos, and so on) or because they heard their views misrepresented from the pulpit or in conversation afterward.

But our churches do not exist only for their members, but for those in our wider communities. While never compromising the truth, we need proactively to welcome everyone with genuine warmth and with concern for their souls. So we are to gather with an eye out for the stranger, the guest, and the person sitting alone. While we come to be strengthened personally, we also come to be a missionary in church.[42]

WHO IS THE GATHERING FOR?

Before thinking about some biblical and practical ways to be more evangelistically minded in our gatherings, we need to pause to ask, "Who is the gathering for?" This has been debated in recent years so, at the risk of over-simplification, let me summarize some of these views.

---

41 https://bible.org/illustration/mahatma-gandhi (accessed Jan. 31, 2022).

42 Tony Merida, *Love Your Church*, p 52.

Some in *attractional* church-growth models (like the "seeker-sensitive" movement) believe that to reach unbelievers we need to design worship to cater primarily to them. Worship should make seekers feel comfortable by providing a non-threatening experience. "Felt need"-based programs should be available, and slick marketing is usually employed. Rarely in such services will one see verse-by-verse preaching through books of the Bible, regular Communion, or talk about hell, God's wrath, or other challenging parts of the gospel. Sermons should address the questions of unbelievers and seek to be "relevant." Worship services should never be boring, and often state-of-the-art technology is employed to garner interest and excitement. Everything from childcare to entering the church building to parking-lot practices are designed to make unbelievers feel welcomed.

Unfortunately, as many in this movement have admitted, the failure in such a philosophy is that it is weak in discipleship. The goal can easily become the size of the crowd rather than the depth of devotion among the saints. Critics claim that many in these contexts have made professions of faith but never had possession of real faith due to the lack of biblical evangelism and discipleship. Others point out that the overemphasis on calling people to buildings and events leads to a lack of attention on Christians being sent out into the world as missionaries.

Then there is the entirely different direction promoted by the "believers-only" camp. They argue that the *only* purpose for the weekly gathering is to edify the saints. Sure, unbelievers may turn up, but that has little to nothing to do with the weekly gathering. Sundays are for discipling God's people. As for "seekers," critics in this camp adamantly oppose this idea, arguing that "no one seeks God" (Romans 3:11)—it is God alone who seeks, finds, and saves.

There is a third way. I believe it is possible to be about both edification and evangelism on Sundays. It is possible to equip insiders and to engage with outsiders. Even though it seems the *primary* focus for the gathering is for *believers*, there are several biblical reasons for remaining evangelistically minded in our public gatherings.

To do this, we need to put ourselves in the shoes of an outsider. This is especially important for new churches as they get older, for established congregations that have increasing internal needs to attend to, and for more long-standing believers, who can easily forget what it was like to be an outsider. Preaching— indeed, everything—should of course aim to build up Christians, but also to speak to non-Christians. Church should be a place to which a church member comes to hear the gospel and invites their friend to hear that same gospel. After all, what both the Christian and non-Christian most need to hear in the sermon and singing, and see in the ordinances and experience in the fellowship, is the gospel!

BE THE WELCOME

Hospitality is not a small thing in the Bible (1 Timothy 3:2; Titus 1:8; Hebrews 13:2; Romans 12:13).[43] Welcoming strangers is a big deal (see Leviticus 19:33-34). As Christians, we know that when we were far off, we were brought near by the blood of Christ (Ephesians 2:11-22), and the proper response to this grace is a life of gracious welcome to others, whoever they are (James 2:1-7).

So, try to remember what it was like to be an unbeliever, or what it is like to attend some event as an outsider, in order to remain sensitive to guests in a way that commends the gospel. Recognize that you have an important role to play. You may be one of the first church members an outsider meets. Take the opportunity to get to know them and to introduce them to others they may have things in common with, and try to get together with them after the service.

UNDERSTANDING MATTERS

Every week, we should pray for unbelievers to come to our corporate gatherings and then act as though they have. The apostle Paul gave us the grand hope that when non-Christians show up, they may sense that "God is among us":

If, therefore, the whole church comes together and all speak in tongues, and outsiders or unbelievers enter,

---

43 See Tony Merida, *Ordinary* (B&H, 2015), chapter 2.

> *will they not say that you are out of your minds? But if*
> *all prophesy, and an unbeliever or outsider enters, he is*
> *convicted by all, he is called to account by all, the secrets*
> *of his heart are disclosed, and so, falling on his face, he*
> *will worship God and declare that God is really among*
> *you. (1 Corinthians 14:23-25)*

Paul calls on the church to consider unbelievers when they gather. He instructs the church to make the service *intelligible* to outsiders. Whether or not you believe in the practice of speaking in tongues today, you can see Paul's point. This call to be clear is certainly a responsibility for those leading the corporate worship services, but one does not have to be in leadership to help ensure gospel clarity. It may be as simple as leaning toward your friend during or after the message and asking if he or she understands what is being communicated. Ask yourself: In your conversations before and after the service, and in anything you do up front, do outsiders understand what we are saying and doing? Are they confused by insider jokes and unclear about Christian jargon? Be pleased when the sermon is preached in such a way that they will understand it, even if that means it is not tailored only to you as a believer.

Yes, only God seeks sinners—but we do not know whom God is seeking! We do not know if he is drawing the outsider in our gatherings. We know the Lord uses means to bring people to faith. And those means include *hearing the word of Christ* (Romans 10:17). This does not mean we water down our message; indeed, such visitors need to hear the whole gospel including sin, judgment, repentance, and so on. But it does mean that we need to be intelligible.

WHAT DO UNBELIEVERS SEE IN US?

Contrary to popular opinion, what people think of us does matter. We should care about what unbelievers see in us.

Paul told the Romans, "Repay no one evil for evil, but give thought to do what is honorable *in the sight of all*" (Romans 12:17, my emphasis). He tells the Thessalonian church to be mindful of outsiders in their daily lives, saying, "Aspire to live quietly, and to mind your own affairs, and to work with your hands, as we instructed you, *so that you may walk properly before outsiders* and be dependent on no one" (1 Thessalonians 4:11-12, my emphasis). Jesus said that we should let our light shine *before others* so that they may see it and glorify our Father (Matthew 5:16).

What do unbelievers see in you? Do they see spiritual pride and arrogance? Do they see indifference? Are they observing division and grumbling? Or do they sense, first, a deep joy for Christ and, second, an authentic love of others?

First, joy. Why would anyone want to be part of something that is lifeless and joyless? A joyful and passionate church is *attractive* in the best sense of the word. One pastor put it this way:

We have an enthusiastic church. I've read the studies that say you can't sing for any longer than seventeen minutes, that messages shouldn't go longer than twenty, and that people are put off by expressiveness. That hasn't been our experience.

When unbelievers visit our church, they find people who are awestruck and amazed by the kindness and mercy of God. And we seek to make it clear that God's grace is what has affected us so deeply. We don't meet just to talk about God; we're encountering his gracious presence. And we aren't reluctant to express outwardly what has so affected us inwardly. People show demonstrative emotion all the time at rock concerts and basketball games and no one ever questions it. Why do we think guests will be surprised to see it in people who claim to have the greatest news the world has ever heard?[44]

As we gather and pour out our praise to God and hear his word with humble and grateful hearts, we convey to our unbelieving friends that Jesus is better than anything this world affords and his salvation is worth celebrating with all our hearts. This means that one way you can be evangelistically minded in worship is by being deeply satisfied in God yourself. A good evangelist is a passionate worshiper. The 20th-century pastor Martyn

---

44 Bob Kauflin, "How to Worship in a Way That Speaks to Unbelievers," https:// www.crossway.org/articles/how-to-worship-in-a-way-that-speaks-to-unbelievers/ (accessed Jan. 18, 2022).

Lloyd-Jones wrote: "The greatest need of the hour is a revived and joyful church ... Unhappy Christians are a poor recommendation for the faith ... The exuberant joy of the early Christians was one of the most potent factors in the spread of Christianity."[45] The gospel joy in you should lead to expressions of passionate adoration that get people's attention. People will see your gospel hope and ask questions as a result (1 Peter 3:15).

Second, love. Recall Jesus' important words:

> Just as I have loved you, you also are to love one another. By this all people will know that you are my disciples, if you have love for one another.
>
> (John 13:34-35)

The charge to love one another as Christ has loved us is not only for the good of fellow believers; it is also for the good of our witness to the watching world.

In The Mark of the Christian, Francis Schaeffer called this act of loving one another "the final apologetic"[46]— it is a powerful way for conveying the validity of our faith. The world will know that we are Jesus' disciples not by our well-crafted statements (as important as they are) or by our smooth-looking worship services but by looking at how you and I love one another (see also John 17:20-21, 23).

---

45 D. Martyn Lloyd-Jones, *Spiritual Depression* (Eerdmans, 1965), p 5.

46 Francis Schaeffer, *The Mark of the Christian* (InterVarsity, 1970).

Christians have the high calling of loving our enemies (Luke 10:25-37), as well as our neighbors (6:27-36), but we must also recognize the kind of impact that our love for one another can have on unbelievers. When we care for each other, forgive each other, confess to each other, and serve one another, it gives unbelievers the opportunity to see how the gospel works. They get to see the great implications of the gospel, and that is a powerful message.

The pastor Mark Dever highlights the role of the congregation in evangelism saying:

> *Our lives, individually and as church congregations, should give credibility to the Gospel we proclaim. This is one of the reasons why church membership is so important. We as a church bear a corporate responsibility to present to the world what it means to be a Christian ... God is glorified not just by our speaking the message but by our actually living consistently with it—not that any of us can live perfectly, but we can at least try to live in a way that commends the Gospel ... Live a life of committed love to other members of your local church, as a fundamental part of your own sanctification and of your evangelistic ministry. Our individual lives alone are not a sufficient witness. Our lives together as church communities are the confirming echo of our witness.*[47]

47 Dever, *Nine Marks of a Healthy Church*, p 115-16.

Many people view Christianity negatively because of what they have heard about Christianity.[48] But when we love one another the way Christ has loved us, we get to show outsiders something altogether different: something attractive and glorious.

ARE OUTSIDERS INVITED TO OTHER EVENTS?

Lives can be changed by a simple invitation after church like "Do you want to go out to eat with us after the service?" Or "Would you like to come to our small-group's cookout on Thursday night?"

For many non-Christians, they need to hear the gospel many times before responding in faith to Jesus. So invite them to dinners, parties, small-group meetings, and other church events. Offer to pick them up before the Sunday gathering.

When you do this, do not view them as a project. The goal is not to boast in evangelistic success. See them as people who are created in God's image. Value them. Listen to them. Love them. Invite them to be in contexts where the gospel is spoken and where the implications of the gospel are lived out.

Your purpose in gathering, then, is not primarily for you (though you need it) or even just for your church family (though they need you). It is for the sake of the lost. They need to hear the gospel as much as you do. Next Sunday,

---

48 Harvey Turner, *Friend of Sinners* (Lucid Book, 2016), p 1.

what would change if you prayed that unbelievers would be present, invited unbelievers you know, and provided a welcome to those who come along which shows them the love of Christ that you have received yourself?

ACTION STEPS

- *Get to know non-Christians.* If we are going to invite our friends and neighbors to church, and ultimately to Jesus, then we need to know some unbelievers! Think about the people in your networks: where you live, where you shop, where you play, where you work. Notice who God has put in your path and seek to get to know them so that you may invite them.

- *Pray for non-Christians.* Pray for specific people by name. Do you have a list of names of unbelievers for whom you are praying?

- *Attend the gatherings with missional alertness.* Consider who is sitting alone. Consider who looks confused; maybe you can help them understand what is being communicated. Pay attention to those in the congregation, though not in a weird, uncomfortable way but in a way that reflects the character of Jesus. Be gracious, kind, welcoming, and attentive. Maybe you can engage in an evangelistic conversation before or after the service. You may be able to direct an outsider to a pastor for a follow-up meeting.

- *Prepare to worship with passion and to express love to your brothers and sisters.* Get your heart ready to worship God, not only because he is worthy of heartfelt adoration but also because unbelievers are present. Further, come ready to see and express care for your brothers and sisters, not only because they are your brothers and sisters who are in need of encouragement and support but also because this kind of love is a powerful apologetic for the life-changing power of the gospel.

- *When engaging with an unbeliever, be interesting, interested, and inviting.* Ask good questions. Listen to them. Be interested in their story. Use your personality and engage with them in an authentic, wise, gospel-focused way, and invite them to future events.

8. GATHERING TO SCATTER

But be doers of the word, and not hearers only,
deceiving yourselves.
James 1:22

I love Waffle House, not least for the plethora of ways in which you can have your hash browns cooked: *scattered, covered, smothered, topped, chunked,* or *diced.* You may not know the difference between each of these options, but every Christian needs a good understanding of the church *gathered* and *scattered.*

The church gathered (the focus of this book) happens when we meet at regular and organized times for edification and worship.[49] The church scattered involves us living out our faith in worshipful obedience in the world.

While Christians hold Sundays as the high point of the week,[50] we have the privilege and responsibility of living out our faith during the week at home, in the public square, and among the nations. Paul told the Romans,

---

49 Jim Shaddix, *The Passion-Driven Sermon* (B&H, 2003), p 132-133.

50 Bob Kauflin, *Worship Matters* (Crossway, 2008), p 210.

"I appeal to you therefore, brothers, by the mercies of God, to present your bodies as a living sacrifice, holy and acceptable to God, which is your spiritual worship" (Romans 12:1). In other words, *all* of life is to be lived as an act of worship unto God. God is certainly worthy of praise in our corporate assemblies. But he is also worthy of worship in everyday life.

As we live in this broken world during the week, it is easy to grow tired and even discouraged. As we deal with challenges in our relationships, we can become disheartened. As we endure spiritual warfare, we can feel weakened. For all these reasons and more, we need to gather. The gathering gives us hope for the weekly battle. We can read the Bible on our own; we can have devotions with our family; we can take a vacation to rest; but we still need encouragement, instruction, and support from the church. The gathering equips us, inspires us, challenges us, and reminds us of our calling to live lives worthy of the gospel as we scatter.

BEING EQUIPPED FOR MINISTRY

Every Christian should be involved in ministry. Paul tells the Ephesians, "And he [Christ] gave the apostles, the prophets, the evangelists, the shepherds and teachers, to equip the saints for the work of ministry, for building up the body of Christ" (Ephesians 4:11-12). God clearly appoints church leaders to prepare and train church members to serve. The gathering is one of the ways in which believers are equipped for service.

The church should have an every-member ministry, since every believer is called by God to care for their brothers and sisters and every member is gifted by the Spirit to serve (1 Peter 4:10; Romans 12:6). As you attend the weekly gathering, do so ready to be built up in your faith and equipped to serve others. As your church offers classes and programs which serve to disciple and equip believers, take advantage of these opportunities as you can. Allow God's word to shape your thoughts and prepare you for Christ-honoring ministry to others during the week ahead.

So what, then, should the scattered church look like?

DOING THE WORD

We must "be doers of the word, and not hearers only, deceiving [ourselves]" (James 1:22). How might we be "hearers only"? First and more obviously, by hearing a sermon and not putting it into practice. But second, and perhaps this is easier to hide, by spending our lives at church groups talking about how to live the Christian life without ever really getting on with doing so beyond church gatherings. Of course there is certainly a place for small groups and training events and conferences, but what is desperately needed in every age is daily obedience to God's word in God's world. This age has been called the information age, but unfortunately, it will not be called the application age. Attend your gatherings and other church groups not only to hear the word and be nourished but to know how best to live it out.

CARING FOR ONE ANOTHER

Pastoral care is not something reserved exclusively for pastors any more than evangelism is reserved for evangelists alone. All of God's people have a role to play. In Galatians 6, Paul shows how Spirit-filled believers should care for one another, which we will do mainly as the scattered church through the week rather than as the gathered church on a Sunday:

> *Brothers, if anyone is caught in any transgression, you who are spiritual should restore him in a spirit of gentleness. Keep watch on yourself, lest you too be tempted. Bear one another's burdens, and so fulfill the law of Christ ... So then, as we have opportunity, let us do good to everyone, and especially to those who are of the household of faith. (Galatians 6:1-2, 10)*

As we scatter from our places of worship, we have the responsibility of caring for those who are caught in sin and for those weighed down by heavy burdens. We will also have opportunities to bless those in our congregation in other ways during the week.[51] The author of Hebrews reminded the church of the need for giving daily exhortations to one another, saying, "But exhort one another *every* day, as long as it is called 'today,' that none of you may be hardened by the deceitfulness of sin" (Hebrews 3:13, my emphasis).

---

51 For a more developed reflection on Galatians 6, see Tony Merida, *Love Your Church* (The Good Book Company, 2021), chapter 4.

These ministries of care require that we remain alert. We need to be *present* at corporate worship and *present* in the life of the church to know who needs our care. This also requires humility, as the ministries of restoration, burden-bearing, and blessing are often not visible to or praised by others. But they matter. Here is a daily mission for all of us: be alert to the burdens of others and seek to ease their burdens in biblical, thoughtful ways.

LIVING HONORABLY IN SOCIETY

Further, our gatherings should equip and inspire us to live honorable lives in a pagan world, as well. Passages like 1 Peter 2:13 – 3:12 show us ways in which we testify to the gospel in society.

Peter was writing to believers who were seeking to live the Christian life in a less-than-ideal situation (after all, Nero was reigning!). After giving the general exhortation to live honorably among unbelievers (2:11-12), he gives specific ways in which "sojourners and exiles" (v 11) can display Christ-centered honor toward governing authorities (v 13-17), in servant-master relationships (v 18-25), in marriage (3:1-7), and in the church (v 8-12). He summarizes this nicely in verse 2:17: "Honor everyone. Love the brotherhood. Fear God. Honor the emperor."

Our gatherings should remind us that we are not home yet. And so, as pilgrims on a journey, we reflect a different set of values and live differently than the world around us. We should be marked by abstaining from the sins of the age (v 11) and marked by "good deeds" (v 12). Peter envisions Christians living this kind of life. As the church scatters, we need to keep these things in mind as we enter the world, which is often raging, divisive, dishonoring, dishonest, and immoral. Being generous, treating people with dignity, doing our work with integrity and discipline, showing honor to leaders, cultivating marital harmony, and maintaining unity in the church are all ways in which we glorify God and commend the gospel. These are beautiful actions and can be very powerful ways to testify to the gospel before a watching world.

DOING JUSTICE AND MERCY

It is one thing to participate in religious events and ceremonies, but it is another to live a life of faithfulness in the ordinary rhythms of life. The prophet Amos spoke God's warning to his people:

> *I hate, I despise your feasts,*
>   *and I take no delight in your solemn assemblies.*
> *Even though you offer me your burnt offerings and*
>   *grain offerings,*
>   *I will not accept them;*
> *and the peace offerings of your fattened animals,*
>   *I will not look upon them.*
> *Take away from me the noise of your songs;*
>   *to the melody of your harps I will not listen.*
> *But let justice roll down like waters,*
>   *and righteousness like an ever-flowing stream.*
>   *(Amos 5:21-24)*

God *hates* their gatherings because of their sinful conduct, their perversion of worship, and the lack of justice and righteousness in their lives. Micah makes the same charge against the people, finishing...

> *He has told you, O man, what is good;*
>   *and what does the LORD require of you*
> *but to do justice, and to love kindness,*
>   *and to walk humbly with your God?*
>   *(Micah 6:8; see also Deuteronomy 10:12-22)*

What does God want? He wants his people to do justice, love kindness, and walk humbly before him. Faithfulness to God consists not in empty ritual but in these proper expressions of love. Our gatherings should inspire and equip us to live such lives of justice and mercy.

Jesus may have been alluding to Micah's text when he rebuked the religious leaders for giving meticulous attention to religious offerings while neglecting matters of justice, love, and faithfulness (Matthew 23:23-24). We are to challenge ourselves (and each other) not to fall into the same hypocrisy. We are not to prioritize the weekly gathering while failing to pursue a daily life of mercy and justice. What might rejecting such hypocrisy look like? It can look like a whole host of actions:

- supporting a single mother

- bringing joy to a widow's heart

- caring for the fatherless

- feeding the hungry

- praying with the hurting

- advocating for the enslaved

- helping the unemployed

- visiting prisoners

- welcoming immigrants

- serving the elderly

- comforting the grieving

- counseling the abused

- tutoring the underprivileged

- ministering to the addicted

- aiding victims of disaster

- providing aftercare for rescued trafficking victims

This is just a short list of ways that we can reflect the mercy and justice of our God to a broken world in need. And as we pursue this kind of life, we do it as an act of worship to our God.

DECLARING GOD'S GLORY AMONG THE NATIONS

While our primary purpose in corporate worship is to exalt our great God, we should also worship with a missionary heart:

Oh sing to the LORD a new song;
   sing to the LORD, all the earth!
Sing to the LORD, bless his name;
   tell of his salvation from day to day.
Declare his glory among the nations,
   his marvelous works among all the peoples!
                                                (Psalm 96:1-3)

The psalmist picks up on the great promise to Abraham that he and his descendants would be a blessing to all the nations of the earth, and the psalm carries the missionary impulse of the biblical story. In our corporate gatherings, we should remember that there are peoples as yet unreached and express a longing for the nations to come to know God through Jesus Christ, and we should scatter to declare to the world that "the Lord reigns" (v 10). I have said to my own church in our gatherings that, "the only thing problematic about our songs today is that there are too many people not singing them." Be sure never to meet with Jesus' people without remembering that Jesus deserves all the worship of all the people in the world, so that as you scatter, you are prompted to tell the good news to your neighbors and to prayerfully support missionaries who are evangelizing others in hard places around the world, always keeping this great eschatological vision in your minds.

This book has been written to show that as God's people we cannot prize our Sunday gatherings highly enough. But we must not prize them to the detriment of the worship of the rest of our lives. God remains God and the gospel remains good on Monday and through the week—so gather with a view to scattering, caring for your church family and living such good lives among your community in the week that you are the means by which God reminds his people of his goodness and reaches out to others with his gospel.

ACTION STEPS

- *Listen to the weekly sermon with the intention of putting the truth to work.* Be a doer and not just a hearer. Be specific about what you are going to think, pray about, or do in the week ahead as a result of what you have heard from God's word.

- *Take advantage of opportunities to be equipped for ministry.* See your church pastors not as those who do the ministry but as those who are tasked with the job of building you up for ministry. Attend classes at church which will help prepare you for service. Consider meeting with a pastor to discuss other means of preparation like courses outside of your church or good books to read, or online training programs.

- *Put Galatians 6 into practice.* Does anyone come to mind when you think of Paul's words here? Is there someone who would benefit from your ministry of restoration or burden-bearing? Is there anyone that you could bless? Take time each week (perhaps on Sunday evening or Monday morning) to identify some people in your congregation that you want to minster to that week. Often, we fail to do Galatians 6 ministry because we do not plan to do it.

- *Reflect God's character by doing deeds of mercy and justice for those in need and reaching out to the lost.* Are there ways in which you can put Micah 6:8 to work this week? If so, then seize those opportunities. Are there people with whom you can seek to share the gospel this week? Pray for an opportunity to do so, and that you will faithfully take that opportunity.

CONCLUSION

There is a peculiar, distinctive glory in the gathering of Christians together. And we regularly need a renewed vision of the church, seeing it from the New Testament's perspective, so that we can appreciate the church's centrality and glory, and our responsibility in it.

Every Christian has a people, a family, to whom they belong. You not only have a new *personal identity* through your union with Christ, but you also have a new *corporate or communal identity* among the people of God. We are part of the universal church throughout the world and in heaven, and we show we are part of that church by identifying and gathering with *a specific group of people locally*. We live out spiritual union with Christ *visibly* through a life of faithfulness and devotion, and we live out our union with other believers *visibly* by our shared life together and in our regular gatherings of worship.

This communal identity is described beautifully in Ephesians 2:12-22. After reminding believers of their previous alienation from God and each other, Paul articulates what Christ has done to reconcile them to God and one another (v 14-18), so that "through him we [all] have access in one Spirit to the Father". And then Paul goes on to give us three pictures of this corporate identity, which is reflected in our gatherings.:

> *So then you are no longer strangers and aliens, but*
> *you are fellow citizens with the saints and members*
> *of the household of God, built on the foundation of*
> *the apostles and prophets, Christ Jesus himself being the*
> *cornerstone, in whom the whole structure, being joined*
> *together, grows into a holy temple in the Lord. In*
> *him you also are being built together into a dwelling*
> *place for God by the Spirit. (Ephesians 2:19-22)*

First, we are no longer spiritual refugees but are *citizens of God's kingdom* (v 19). US presidents often begin their presidential addresses by saying, "My fellow Americans…" I may or may not like the speech that follows, or the policies of that president, but I have always loved that moment because it says that he is talking to me and that I'm an American. Now imagine Jesus Christ saying to you and me, "My fellow citizens of the kingdom of God."[52] Astonishing! And yet he does. If you are in Christ, you really are a full kingdom citizen, with all the privileges that come with that. Our gatherings put this glorious reality on display.

---

52 Sinclair Ferguson, "The Church as God's Family," https://www.monergism.com/topics/sermon-manuscripts-mp3s-scripture/ephesians/audio-and-mulitmedia/chapter-expositions-1 (accessed Feb. 15, 2022).

Second, *we are members of a family*. Paul calls the believers in Ephesus "members of the household of God" (v 19). It is extraordinary enough that despite all their dislike of each other, Jew and Gentile could be brought together in one kingdom, but to be *one family* is stunning! We are adopted children of God (1:5). Your church is made up of adopted brothers and sisters who love you and who you are to love. Your church is family to whom you belong. So never treat the church as a hotel—visiting it occasionally, giving a tip if you are served well. It's family. Our gatherings put this reality on display as well.

Third, we are *stones in God's temple* (2:20-22). For nearly 1,000 years, the temple had been a focal point for Israel—from Solomon to Zerubbabel to Herod. Now there is a new temple, made up of people. The foundation of the temple is God's word (v 20). Jesus is its cornerstone—he gives security and alignment to the building and is the one on whom everything is built. As his people, we are carefully-shaped building blocks, fitted to build this temple. Paul says that, through Christ, by the work of the Spirit, there is a better temple than any physical building anywhere in the world, made from people from every tribe and tongue, who may have nothing in common except the only thing that eternally matters—faith in Christ. We put this glorious reality on display in our gatherings.

This is why the New Testament has no category for a Christian who does not go to or care much about their local church gathering. That is to be a stone apart from a building or a child separated from their family or a refugee away from their country.[53] God intends for us to live out our faith and to love one another in community. The good news of the gospel has not only changed our personal identity; it has changed our communal identity as well.

And by God's grace, our local gatherings will change the world. My friend Adam Muhtaseb is a former Muslim. He is now a church-planting pastor in Baltimore, Maryland. He loves to share how he was won to faith not through gimmicks but by the power of this gospel. He writes:

In a mosque, there's no fancy stage, no Hillsong United Muslim songs, no mood lighting. The world's fastest growing religion doesn't try to lure people with entertainment. They believe Allah and the Quran's message are compelling enough. Muslims win people to their faith through their message. A 1,500-year-old message from a still-dead prophet seems to be enough. Islam offers a religious to-do list that might help you avoid the fires of hell if you live a good enough life. That's their message, and it scared me enough to keep [me] going. But what brought me to Jesus wasn't fear or a church's bells and whistles. It was a better message. It was the gospel. When Islam choked me with "Do, do, do," Jesus said "It's already done" and captured

---

53 Tony Merida, *Exalting Jesus in Ephesians* (B&H, 2014), p 65.

*my heart. That's how a Muslim kid eventually became
a Christian church planter in one of America's most
unreached cities.*[54]

Person by person, stone by stone, God is building his church. And he will continue to do so. Bible teacher Alistair Begg tells this story about the place of the church in God's purposes and in his world:

*In the 1920s, Lord Reith helped to establish the BBC—
the British Broadcasting Corporation—and then from
1927 served as its first Director-General. He was a
somewhat severe man from the highlands of Scotland.
As the BBC began to be carried along by the tide of
secularism that swept through Britain in the sixties, a
young producer stood up in a meeting and said to Lord
Reith that the world was changing, and that the BBC
did not need to continue with its religious programming
output. People were no longer interested in it, he said,
and the church was becoming increasingly obsolete.*

*Lord Reith, who was 6'6 (2m) tall, stood up, told this
young man to take a seat, and said: "The church will
stand at the grave of the BBC."*[55]

Indeed, it will. It will stand when every news outlet dies. It will stand when every organization and institution

---

54 Adam Muhtaseb, "The Secret to Church Planting (From a Former Muslim),"
https://www.thegospelcoalition.org/article/secret-church-planting/ (accessed
Feb. 3, 2022).

55 Alistair Begg, *Brave by Faith* (The Good Book Company, 2021), p 43.

and empire ends! After all, it is Jesus' church, and he promised, "I will build my church, and the gates of Hades will not overpower it" (Matthew 16:18). What a privilege to belong to the church! Your local gathering may look rather unimpressive to the outside world. Your building may or may not be extraordinary looking. But your gospel is extraordinary. It is the power of God unto salvation (Romans 1:16). The message of Christ is still winning people to faith and uniting diverse believers. As you gather with your brothers and sisters this week, recognize the privilege that you enjoy as a citizen of heaven, a member of the family, and a stone in the temple, and prioritize the activities of the gathering as you stir up one another, as you hear the word, as you sing and pray together, as you take the bread and the cup, and as you witness baptisms. Allow the good news to lead you to adoration, and compel you to mission, as you scatter in Jesus' name.

All in view of the glorious gathering that is to come.

DISCUSSION GUIDE
FOR SMALL GROUPS

1. THE GIFT OF GATHERING

1. *Read Hebrews 10:19-25*. What does the writer say about what Jesus has done and what role he has? What does the writer say about the impact of that on us?

2. What motivates you to worship? Do you agree that "Jesus' work alone enables and motivates our worship and obedience" (p 24)? What would our relationship with God be like if it weren't for Jesus?

3. What does it look like to worship wholeheartedly, sincerely, and passionately?

4. In the chapter, Merida wrote about the impact on us of gathering together in worship. We remind each other of the gospel, and this should bring us joy, confidence, hope, and perseverance. What aspect of your church gatherings helps you the most with these things?

5. What could you personally do to help others in your church draw near to God and persevere in hope?

6. Read the Action Steps on p 33-34. Some of these things might be your practice already. If so, what has their impact been? If not, which would you like to try?

2. GATHERING TO STIR UP ONE ANOTHER

1. When have you been most encouraged by a conversation you've had at a church gathering? Why?

2. Why is physical embodiment so important? Look at what Merida says about this on p 37-38. In what ways does that tally with your own experience?

3. *Read Hebrews 3:12-13.* Why is exhorting each other so crucial, according to these verses? What do you think the writer has in view when he uses the word "exhort" (or "encourage") here—what kinds of encouragement will stop us being hardened by the deceitfulness of sin?

4. Practically speaking, what's the difference between attending church gatherings purely for our own sake and attending with the specific purpose of encouraging and stirring up one another?

5. One of the Action Steps at the end of the chapter talks about having gospel-centered conversations. How easy do you find it to turn to spiritual matters in your conversations before and after a church gathering? Can you think of some questions you could ask that would be really helpful for those you're talking to?

6. What is one thing you'll do this Sunday to encourage someone?

3. GATHERING TO HEAR GOD'S WORD

1. What do you think people in your church would say about the point of preaching? What does Merida say it is?

2. *Read Nehemiah 8:1-12.* What phrases in verses 1-5 tell us about the people's attitude toward God's word? What impact does it have on them in verses 6-12?

3. If you could be more like the people in Nehemiah 8 in one respect, what would it be?

4. How easy do you find it to listen attentively to the Sunday sermon and to understand what's being said? What practical steps do you think would help you with this? (Have a look at the Action Steps on p 56.)

5. How could you get better at remembering what is said on a Sunday and applying it to your own life? (Again, look at the Action Steps for some ideas to start you off.)

6. Based on Nehemiah 8, and on what you've read in chapter 2 of *Gather*, why do you think it is important to hear God's word preached publicly, not just to read it privately?

4. GATHERING TO SING TOGETHER

1. *Read Philippians 2:6-11.* This passage may have been part of a song sung by early Christians. How would you sum up these verses in ordinary language? What is the effect of putting them into poetic language like this?

2. Why do you think singing has such an impact on us?

3. What would you say to someone who said they didn't enjoy the singing in church, or even avoided it?

4. *Read Luke 1:46-55.* What do you think Mary means when she says, "My soul magnifies the Lord"? How would you put that into your own words?

5. In our own singing, how can we put into practice the four things Merida highlighted about Mary's song (see p 64)?

6. What is one thing that will help you to sing with your heart, not just with your lips?

5. GATHERING TO PRAY TOGETHER

1. Look up some of the examples of prayers in the book of Acts (listed on p 69-70). What would it look like for you to imitate each of those examples?

2. Think about the four benefits of corporate prayer highlighted in the chapter. Did any of them surprise you? Which is the most important benefit to you personally, or to your church, at the moment?

3. What is special about praying together as opposed to on your own? What is special about praying out loud instead of in your head?

4. What do you think it looks like to fully participate in corporate prayer, even if you are not the one leading the prayers?

5. How did prayer contribute to revival in the 18th century (see p 73-74)? What will you commit to praying for today's church?

6. What do you need prayer for today? Put the final two Action Steps into practice together. Try using one of the psalms mentioned on p 68.

6. GATHERING TO CELEBRATE THE GOSPEL IN THE ORDINANCES

1. *Read Matthew 28:18-20.* What does Jesus command? Where do we see the theme of commitment and loyalty in his commands?

2. *Read 1 Corinthians 11:22-28.* Why do we celebrate the Lord's Supper, according to these verses?

3. Why is it important to examine ourselves before we come to the Lord's Supper? How can we do this without losing sight of the fact that we are saved by grace alone?

4. Have you heard people make any of the objections listed on p 80-81? What would you say to such a person about the importance of these ordinances, or sacraments?

5. What do you tend to focus on most when you celebrate the Lord's Supper—your sin, Jesus' forgiveness, your unity with other believers, our future in glory, or something else? Are there any aspects you forget? How could you keep reminding yourself of the significance of this meal?

6. How much of an impact do baptism and the Lord's Supper have on you? What is so impactful about them? Or, if you don't find them impactful, how might you recover a sense of awe when you see or participate in these practices?

7. GATHERING TO REACH OUTSIDERS

1. What are the problems with seeing church gatherings as mainly for outsiders or as only for believers (see p 94-96)?

2. *Read John 17:20-26*. Jesus is praying for his disciples—including us. According to this prayer, what will cause unbelievers ("the world") to believe in Jesus? What is our role, what is Jesus' role, and what is the Father's role?

3. In the chapter, Merida discussed various ways in which the way we behave can commend the gospel to outsiders (see especially p 99-103). In what ways do you think you and/or your church are doing this well? Where do you see potential for growth?

4. What kinds of people are there living in the community around your church? Consider the four key points in this chapter (put yourself in the shoes of outsiders; make the service intelligible; care about what unbelievers see in us; invite them to other events) and how you could apply those to your particular community.

5. How confident are you to invite outsiders to church? Spend some time planning how you could invite some unbelievers you know.

6. If you think of yourself as a missionary at church, how will it change your attitudes and behaviors before, during, and after the gathering?

8. GATHERING TO SCATTER

1. *Read 1 Peter 2:9-12.* Why are we still "the church" when we are scattered (not just a bunch of separate individual believers)? What's our purpose as the church, according to verse 9?

2. Why are actions of justice and care for others an act of worship? In what sense do they glorify God?

3. On p 110-111 and p 117, Merida discusses different ways of caring for other believers. How can we care for those who are caught in sin, in particular? How do the verses quoted from Galatians 6 help us to have the right attitude here?

4. Do you think of yourself as being "in ministry"? Which of the ministries outlined by this chapter do you think you are already doing? What would you like to do more of?

5. Do you think your church gatherings help you to live a life that honors God throughout the week? What steps could you take to help yourself carry what is done and said at church gatherings into your daily life?

6. Who could you care for, stand up for, pray for, or share the gospel with this week?

RESOURCES FOR SMALL GROUPS

Access the free small-group kit at loveyourchurchseries. com. The free kit includes a video introduction to each session as well as downloadable PDFs of a discussion guide and worksheets. Each session is based on a chapter of the book.

loveyourchurchseries.com

BIBLIOGRAPHY

Christopher Ash, *Teaching Psalms* (Christian Focus, 2017)

Augustine, *Confessions*, Translated with an Introduction and Notes by Henry Chadwick (Oxford University Press, 1991)

Gregg R. Allison, *The Church: An Introduction* (Wheaton: Crossway, 2021)

Gregg R. Allison, *Sojourners and Strangers* (Wheaton: Crossway, 2012)

Charitie Lees Bancroft, "Before the Throne of God Above," https://hymnary.org/text/before_the_throne_of_god_above_i_have_a_ (accessed Dec. 16, 2022).

Alistair Begg, *Brave by Faith* (The Good Book Company, 2021)

Mike Bird, *Romans*, The Story of God Bible Commentary (Grand Rapids: Zondervan, 2016)

Dietrich Bonhoeffer, *Life Together* (Harper One, 1954)

F.F. Bruce, *The Book of Acts*, the New International Commentary on the New Testament (Eerdmans, 1988)

Arnold. Dallimore, *George Whitefield*, Vol. 1 (The Banner of Truth Trust, 2001)

Mark Dever, *Nine Marks of a Healthy Church* (Crossway, 2000)

Ligon Duncan, "What Shall We Wear to Church." Sermon online at https://ligonduncan.com/what-shall-we-wear-to-church-719/. Accessed Jan 25, 2022.

Sinclair Ferguson, "The Church as God's Family," https://www.monergism.com/topics/sermon-manuscripts-mp3s-scripture/ephesians/audio-and-mulitmedia/chapter-expositions-1 (accessed Feb. 15, 2022).

Richard Foster, *Celebration of Discipline* (Harper Collins, 1998)

Micah Fries, "Exalting Jesus in Zephaniah, Haggai, Zechariah, Malachi," *Christ-Centered Exposition Commentary* (B&H, 2015)

"Mahatma Gandhi," https://bible.org/illustration/mahatma-gandhi (accessed Jan. 31, 2022).

Stanley J. Grenz, *The Baptist Congregation* (Regent College Publishing, 1985)

Jim Hamilton, "A Biblical Theology for Corporate Prayer," https://www.9marks.org/article/biblical-theology-corporate-prayer/ (accessed Dec. 30, 2021).

R. Kent Hughes, *Hebrews*, Preaching the Word (Wheaton: Crossway, 1993)

R. Kent Hughes and Bryan Chappell, *1 & 2 Timothy and Titus* (Crossway, 2000)

Bob Kauflin, "How to Worship in a Way That Speaks to Unbelievers," https://www.crossway.org/articles/how-to-worship-in-a-way-that-speaks-to-unbelievers/ (accessed Jan. 18, 2022).

Bob Kauflin, *Worship Matters* (Crossway, 2008)

Tim Keller with Kathy Keller, *The Songs of Jesus* (Penguin, 2015)

William L. Lane, *Hebrews 9-13,* Word Biblical Commentary (Word Books, 1991)

C.S. Lewis, "Reflections on the Psalms," *The Inspirational Writings of C.S. Lewis* (Inspirational Press, 1994)

D. Martyn Lloyd-Jones, *Spiritual Depression* (Eerdmans, 1964)

Tony Merida, *Exalting Jesus in Ephesians* (B&H, 2014)

Tony Merida, *Exalting Jesus in Romans* (B&H, 2021)

Tony Merida, *Love Your Church* (The Good Book Company, 2021)

Tony Merida, *Ordinary* (B&H, 2015)

Tony Merida, *The Christ-Centered Expositor* (B&H, 2016)

Adam Muhtaseb, "The Secret to Church Planting (From a Former Muslim)," https://www.thegospelcoalition.org/article/secret-church-planting/ (accessed Feb. 3, 2022).

Peter T. O'Brien, *The Letter to the Ephesians*, Pillar New Testament Commentary (Eerdmans, 2010)

John Onwuchekwa, *Prayer: How Praying Together Shapes the Church* (Crossway, 2018)

Andrew Pettegree, *Brand Luther* (Penguin, 2016)

Richard D. Phillips, *Hebrews* (P&R, 2006)

John Piper, "A Peculiar Act of Worship," https://www.desiringgod.org/messages/a-peculiar-act-of-worship (accessed Dec. 7, 2021).

John Piper, *The Pleasures of God*, Revised Edition (Multnomah, 2015)

Philip Graham Ryken, Derek W.H. Thomas, and J. Ligon Duncan III, eds, *Give Praise to God* (P&R, 2003)

Francis Schaeffer, *The Mark of the Christian* (InterVarsity, 1970)

Jim Shaddix, *The Passion-Driven Sermon* (B&H, 2003)

Charles Spurgeon, "Difficulty in the Way of

Believing," https://archive.spurgeon.org/misc/wg.php#Difficulty%20in%20the%20Way%20of%20Believing (accessed Dec. 7, 2021).

Charles Spurgeon, "The Power of Prayer and the Pleasure of Praise," https://ccel.org/ccel/spurgeon/sermons09/sermons09.xxi.html (accessed Dec. 30, 2021).

John R.W. Stott, *Guard the Truth* (InterVarsity, 1996)

John R.W. Stott, *The Message of Acts* (InterVarsity Press, 1990)

John R.W. Stott, *The Message of Ephesians* (InterVarsity Press, 1979)

Paul Tripp, *Do You Believe?* (Crossway, 2021)

Harvey Turner, *Friend of Sinners* (Lucid Books, 2016)

Kevin Vanhoozer, *Hearers and Doers* (Lexham, 2019)

Ray Van Neste, "The Lord's Supper in the Context of the Local Church," *The Lord's Supper* (B&H, 2010)

Robert E. Webber, *Ancient-Future Worship* (Baker, 2008)

Donald Whitney, *Spiritual Disciplines for the Christian Life* (NavPress, 2014)

Don Williams, "Psalms 73-150," *The Preacher's Commentary* (Thomas Nelson, Kindle Edition, 1989)

LOVE YOUR CHURCH

thegoodbook.com
thegoodbook.co.uk

thegoodbook
COMPANY

BIBLICAL | RELEVANT | ACCESSIBLE

At The Good Book Company, we are dedicated to helping Christians and local churches grow. We believe that God's growth process always starts with hearing clearly what he has said to us through his timeless word—the Bible.

Ever since we opened our doors in 1991, we have been striving to produce Bible-based resources that bring glory to God. We have grown to become an international provider of user-friendly resources to the Christian community, with believers of all backgrounds and denominations using our books, Bible studies, devotionals, evangelistic resources, and DVD-based courses.

We want to equip ordinary Christians to live for Christ day by day, and churches to grow in their knowledge of God, their love for one another, and the effectiveness of their outreach.

Call us for a discussion of your needs or visit one of our local websites for more information on the resources and services we provide.

Your friends at The Good Book Company

thegoodbook.com | thegoodbook.co.uk
thegoodbook.com.au | thegoodbook.co.nz
thegoodbook.co.in